THE
BUCK
STOPS
HERE

Ashutosh Garg, an MBA, has worked in the corporate sector for twenty-five years. He was with ITC Limited for seventeen years, leaving in 1995 as managing director of one of the group companies. In April 2003, he started a chain of health and beauty retail outlets under the name Guardian Pharmacy. Since 2006, he has been a director of the GAVI Alliance. A member of the Retail Strategy Council of India, he has also served on the advisory council of The Centre for Policy Research and continues to serve on the boards of several companies. He has been a regular contributor to publications such as *Business India* and *The Economic Times*, and is the author of *The Corner Office*. You can reach him on Twitter at @gargashutosh or email him at tbsh@ashutoshgarg.in

Praise for the book:

'Ashutosh is an unusually intrepid entrepreneur [...] We need to see Ashutosh's book as a bit of social history, not just as a management guide, which it most certainly is. Well-written limpid prose makes it a sure eye-catcher.'
      —Jerry Rao, former chairman, NASSCOM and former CEO, MphasiS

'Ashutosh Garg found his calling in the pharmacy retail business and I am delighted to see his success. This book outlines his journey and I am confident that the pointers in the book will help the readers.'
      —Sanjeev Bikhchandani, founder, Naukri.com

'That he is willing to share his story about leaving the corporate life to build his own business is a great opportunity for managers and entrepreneurs everywhere, and I predict his book will become a must-read for anyone considering that transition.'

—George W. Wellde, former vice chairman, Goldman Sachs

'Many of us professionals have dreamt of doing this, but Ashutosh demonstrated the courage to cross the line and realize his dream.'

—Raj Jain, CEO, Bharti Retail Ltd

'Ashutosh Garg's latest effort has all the potential of a bestseller. I shall be watching his journey as an author with great interest.'

—Sanjiv Goenka, chairman, RP-Sanjiv Goenka Group

'I don't know of too many people who have successfully transitioned into becoming entrepreneurs and especially in a new unknown field. Ashutosh ventured into the unknown with a pioneering and passionate spirit.'

—Rajeev Bakshi, managing director, Metro Cash & Carry

'If anyone wants to be an entrepreneur, this is the time to take the jump. And if you needed a handbook to psyche yourself...here is one that will help you...'

—Muralidhara Kadaba, former country manager,
American Express India

'...the story and the journey should be an example that helps other professionals navigate their way to more fulfilling and impactful roles in the India of tomorrow.'

—Raj Mitta, former chairman, Arthur D. Little Inc.

'The Buck Stops Here offers valuable insights into the journey from an MNC executive to a successful startup. It is a must read for every successful large company executive who hopes to turn entrepreneur one day!'

—Pavan Vaish, global COO, UnitedLex Corporation

THE BUCK STOPS HERE

LEARNINGS OF A #STARTUP ENTREPRENEUR

ASHUTOSH GARG

RUPA

Published by
Rupa Publications India Pvt. Ltd 2014
7/16, Ansari Road, Daryaganj
New Delhi 110002

Sales Centres:
Allahabad Bengaluru Chennai
Hyderabad Jaipur Kathmandu
Kolkata Mumbai

First published in India by Penguin Books 2011
This revised edition first published by Rupa Publications India Pvt. Ltd 2014

ISBN: 978-81-291-2369-5

First impression 2014

10 9 8 7 6 5 4 3 2 1

The moral right of the author has been asserted.

Printed by Gopsons Papers Ltd., Noida

To my wife, Vera,
and my sons, Varun and Ashwin,
without whom my journey would have been incomplete

Contents

PREFACE

Why can't a 'bania' play hockey or football for India?
Because every time he gets a corner, he opens a shop!

—Old Indian Joke

Everyone has a story to tell. This is mine.

Everyone's life is full of unique experiences. Each one of us has faced joys and sorrows, pain and exhilaration, and has learned lessons in life. Yet, most people I know are shy of sharing their rich experience.

I often ask such people what they have learned from their life and why they don't wish to share their knowledge with others. After all, it is only when we learn to confront our own 'ghosts' that we will be able to really look back at our lives with confidence, joy and pride.

I have lived my life on my own terms. I have been called a maverick by friends and colleagues and I know that I would not have lived my life any other way.

This book is an attempt to share my personal journey from a professional manager to an entrepreneur over the last thirty-one years.

Many people live their lives working in one job and retiring from the same organization. Others get a chance to change jobs, but stay within the same space. As the years go by and as our societies and the communities will evolve further, I believe that the world will offer our children an opportunity not just to change jobs but to change their careers and their lives completely. Our children can now dream of working in the corporate sector or the government, then move to pursue their passion as a musician or an actor or an author and later enter politics or contribute to civil society, all in one lifetime.

I believe I have been more fortunate than a lot of others to have seen three completely different phases in my life—seventeen years with ITC Limited till I was thirty-eight years old, eight years in the aerospace industry till I was forty-six and the last ten years as a chemist, or in more glorious terms, an entrepreneur.

This book is an account of my journey through life as I built Guardian Pharmacy. In order to do justice to my entrepreneurial journey, I thought that it is also very important to share some of the experiences of the first twenty-five years of my life as a corporate manager. It is this strong foundation and varied experience in the corporate sector that helped me set up the base and develop the mindset to pursue my dream of becoming an entrepreneur. I have also written about the various predicaments I have faced throughout my life and how these learnings from them have made me a much stronger person.

I started out with a dream to build India's largest pharmacy chain. It has now evolved into India's second largest chain of wellness, health and beauty stores with over two hundred stores spread across thirty cities and ten states. We handle over eight million customers every year and have grown at a compounded average annual growth rate of over 40 per cent over the last five years.

Over the last few years, I have met hundreds of professional managers who have expressed their desire to start off on their own. Some have told me in no uncertain terms, 'We are jealous of you since you have managed to break free from the corporate world.'

When I ask them what was stopping them from leaving their jobs to pursue their dream, I heard all kinds of excuses:

'I have too many financial commitments at the moment.'

'I am not used to working on weekends.'

'I don't know what to do, give me a good idea.'

'Is this really a good time to start?'

And the mother of all reasons,

'My family and I have got used to a certain standard of life. I cannot give all this up at this stage.'

My advice to all of them is simple: take the plunge and start your planning process now. There is no day as good as today to make a beginning, if you genuinely believe in your dream. Building a new company is very hard work. The toughest part of building a new company is not coming up with a new idea; it is to stay committed to your dream, make sacrifices and learn from your experiences. If you are not willing to give up on things really important to you or if you are likely to be discouraged because of rejection, it will be very difficult to stick to and implement your idea.

As a first-generation entrepreneur, I did not have anyone to guide me on the dos and don'ts of building a business. Since the time I started Guardian, I have stumbled many times, fallen down quite often, but I have had to build the resilience to stand up, dust my clothes, learn from the mistake and start all over again. I learned to fail and I learned to manage failure, though I did not plan failure.

Failure is essential for any new entrepreneur to succeed. We cannot let any adversity pull us back. We have to learn from our mistakes and our setbacks, accept the knocks our profit-and-loss account will take and keep moving ahead. Every entrepreneur has to plan for the best but prepare for the worst.

I have often heard the phrase, 'The buck stops here.'

I have also used this phrase innumerable times as a professional chief executive officer (CEO) in a large company, implying that I am the final decision-maker and that the responsibility of all my actions and those of others reporting to me finally ends up on my table.

My understanding of this phrase has evolved during my entrepreneurial journey. An entrepreneur is the only person where the proverbial 'buck' stops. At the end of each month, he has to have the money to pay employees' salaries and he has to ensure that there are no delays in doing so.

In November 2009, as I concluded my talk at a large conference on entrepreneurship and building a new business, I was surrounded by dozens of young men and women who wanted to exchange business cards with me so that they could set up a separate meeting to discuss their business plans.

Some of these young men and women came to my office and I spent half a day with them, talking about my journey as I built Guardian, as well as my transition from the corporate world to an entrepreneur. At this meeting I was asked many questions, some perceptive and some very basic, about building a business. As I answered these queries, I thought it may be a good idea for me to write about my own journey so that I could share my knowledge with a much larger audience.

The first edition of this book was released on 10 January 2011 by Mr Omar Abdullah, honourable chief minister of Jammu and Kashmir. It went on to become a bestseller. This is a revised edition, which includes several new thoughts and experiences of mine since the first edition was published.

Writing this book has been a very therapeutic journey for me. I hope you will enjoy reading this book as much as I have enjoyed writing it.

WHO IS AN ENTREPRENEUR?

*In oneself lies the whole world and if you know how to look
and learn, the door is there and the key is in your hand.
Nobody on earth can give you either the key or the door to
open, except yourself.*

—Jiddu Krishnamurthi

So exactly who is an entrepreneur?

In a broad sense, an entrepreneur is a person who:

1. Organizes a business venture and assumes the risk for it.
2. Has looked at a problem and seen it as an opportunity or a likely prospect to start something new.
3. Feels that his ambition is being held in check by corporate red tape. Though it takes more than just cleverness and frustration with the status quo to get an entrepreneurial venture off the ground.
4. Assumes the financial risk of the initiation, operation and management of a business.

Most entrepreneurs are driven not by the need to make money, but by the desire to make their dreams a reality. More often than not, money is the by-product of an entrepreneur's motivation, rather than the motivation itself. Entrepreneurs are not observers but participants; players, not fans. To be an entrepreneur is to be an optimist, to believe that with the right amount of time and money, you can achieve anything.

An entrepreneur's 'gut feeling' is often the subject of a lot of discussion, and my own learning here has been that gut feeling is really the extract of one's own experience or the leanings from someone else's experience, and one's ability for risk-taking rather than some vision that an entrepreneur purportedly has had.

When I was asked in an interview whether I gambled at a casino, I said that I bet the house every day in my business and therefore do not find a casino exciting enough. As Vera, my wife, puts it, 'You are a risk-taker, not a gambler.'

Contrary to popular belief, entrepreneurs aren't generally high risk-takers if they can't influence the outcome of the situation. They tend to set realistic and achievable goals, and when they do take risks, they do so based on facts and experience, rather than instincts.

ME, ENTREPRENEUR?

When you reach an obstacle, turn it into an opportunity.
You have the choice.
You can overcome and be a winner, or you can allow it to
overcome you and be a loser.
The choice is yours and yours alone.
Refuse to throw in the towel. Go that extra mile that failures
refuse to travel.
It is far better to be exhausted from success than to be rested
from failure.

—Mary Kay Ash, founder, Mary Kay Cosmetics

1 April 2003

I woke up with a feeling of uncertainty at 6 a.m. on April Fool's Day. Born on 30 September 1956, I was exactly forty-six years and six months old.

I had given up twenty-five years of corporate life and broken free from the shackles of daily routine. After an MBA from one of India's top business schools and twenty-five years of work experience, with the last decade being spent in jobs at the very top of the corporate sector, I had, with one stroke of my pen, resigned from my job and joined the growing ranks of the 'educated unemployed'.

I had no job and no security of a monthly pay cheque. I

had no office and no secretary. I had no reason to get ready in the morning, no place to go to and nothing planned for the day ahead. My Outlook calendar, which used to drive my daily schedule, was blank.

I have always been a very driven individual with a strong desire to excel at whatever I do. I have believed in my ability to do most tasks without too much reliance on anyone else, but giving up on everything was a completely different experience. I realized what strong emotional strength one's colleagues provided and how important it was for every human being to have the support infrastructure that a workplace offered. I had taken for granted my mid-morning coffee with fellow workers or my lunch in the staff cafeteria while discussing the goings-on in our professional and, at times, personal lives.

Now that I had decided to make a clean break from working as an 'employee', the desire to take a day off to play golf, or put my feet up and watch TV, or just take a break did not seem that exciting any longer. I had to figure out a way to keep myself occupied.

Self-doubt started to creep in.

Had I taken the right decision to stop working, quit the corporate world and give up the comfort of a regular monthly pay cheque, along with all the associated benefits? My sons were going to start college education in a few months and my financial commitments would go up drastically. Had I earned enough to support my family?

Was it safe to start to dip into my life savings at this age? Was I too old to even consider becoming an entrepreneur? Did I have it in me to do so? Did I have the right to gamble with my family's future and use our savings to pursue my dream?

It is easy to get used to the lifestyle a large company

affords to its senior management, specially its expatriate top management. Managers tend to forget the amount of credibility the brand name of their organization gives; I have often met managers who assume that they are bigger than their company. Having worked as a manager for ITC Limited for seventeen years and then spent eight years in the aerospace business, was I equipped to start my own venture?

From travelling first class on international flights and business class on domestic flights and staying in the best hotels around the world, would I be able to adjust to flying economy class and staying in lower-rung hotels that I could afford? Would I be able to travel without all the frills associated with business travel?

Was I in a position to start from the ground up, all over again?

◆

The thought of starting on my own took root in early 2002, when I began to feel the need to cut down on my hectic lifestyle. I was travelling almost twenty days a month and it had started to take its toll on my physical and mental health. I had started to mix up hotel room numbers as I travelled from one city to another. The final straw was when I was lying in bed in a hotel room in Seoul, staring at the ceiling and not being able to recall the city I was in!

Actually, the seeds of starting my own business had been sowed when my family and I had moved back to Delhi from Singapore in 1996. McDonalds had just started operations in India. I contacted them and we had a number of discussions on the possibility of their giving me the franchise for either south India or east India. Vera and I liked the possibility of taking a McDonalds franchise. Both of us also worked at a McDonalds store in east Delhi for two days to understand the business. However, we did not get beyond the training stage because neither of us enjoyed working in the restaurant business.

A few years later, continuing my search to 'do something of my own', I signed a Memorandum of Understanding with Délifrance, Singapore, to open coffee, sandwich and bakery retail outlets. This was before Barista and Café Coffee Day had started operations in India. After spending some time with them in Singapore, once again I realized that food service and perishable products were not something I would enjoy managing or working with.

As a child, one of my favourite authors was Enid Blyton, and I used to devour the Famous Five series and the Noddy books written by her. While these books were available in English in India, there was no translation into Hindi or into any other Indian language, thus depriving a large number of Indian children from their fascinating worlds. This was another venture Vera and I worked on in 1998. We decided to explore the opportunity of taking Hindi and other Indian language rights for Enid Blyton books and television shows. I spent several weeks with the owners of the brand in London and we agreed to move forward. Unfortunately, the brand got sold and our discussions came to a standstill.

Thereafter, I decided to try my luck as an angel investor. I invested my money over a couple of years during the dotcom boom, like so many of my friends, but I did not get involved in running any of these businesses. I invested money in other people's dreams. At one stage, I had also invested in a software company and a portal on religion. Some of these businesses did well and some did not. However, personally, I lost money!

Did I have it in me to start a green-field venture and run it successfully?

And yet, there had always been this long-pending desire to do something of my own and be 'my own boss', which was why I had decided to quit the corporate world in the first place. Over the period 1996 to 2003, I had looked at many opportunities, either as an angel investor or as a direct business venture, but I had not had the courage to 'break away' from the comfort of a top management job in a multinational company. I had to convince myself that now was the right time to do so.

Much later, after I had started Guardian Pharmacy, my secretary, Rajni Kalra, would tell me that my wife and she used to talk quite often over the phone, wondering, 'How will Mr Garg be able to run a house, pay the children's college fees and the office bills by selling Crocin tablets?'

It took some time to convince my wife that though I was taking the plunge so late in life, I had set aside adequate funds to ensure that if nothing worked, we would still be able to maintain a lifestyle similar to what we had. Further, both my sons had full scholarships. The money I had set aside for their education was now also available for my entrepreneurial ambitions.

Rajni, who has worked with me for several years in the corporate world, used to feel sorry for me in the early days of starting Guardian. When I got my first office table, which was three feet wide and two feet long, she came into my room and said that she had never seen me sit at such a small table. When she saw me standing behind the counter of my first store, she asked me how I could possibly think that I had taken the right decision in leaving the corporate world.

But whatever her misgivings about my dream, Rajni stood by my side through all the issues we faced in building the company. Now she says: 'I want to make Guardian the number one pharmacy retail chain in India.'

My son Ashwin once asked me on one of his trips back home from Canada, 'Pop, how can you build a business waiting for people to fall sick?'

He was right. For many months I used to wonder if I had made the right choice to start a company which would make money from people who were unwell. Even when I wrote my first business plan, I found it strange to estimate how many people would fall sick when the weather changed so that we could get revenues, or estimate how much money we would make by selling medicines to an oncology or nephrology patient.

I knew that I was venturing into an area I had very little knowledge of. However, I did have a lot of varied experience in my early years that I would draw upon consistently, and I had plenty of confidence in myself. My legs were not very young but they were not old either, and the word 'tired' did not exist in my dictionary.

Life is not what you want it to be. Life is what you make it.

Why Pharmacy Retail?

India is a nation of shopkeepers. With over fifteen million outlets, India's retail sector is highly fragmented. Less than 4 per cent of the outlets are bigger than 500 square feet in area and the remaining 96 per cent are primarily in the unorganized sector. Out of this, one of the major retail segments is the ubiquitous 'chemist'. We can find a medicine shop at every corner of every village and city in our country under different descriptions ranging from druggists and chemists to drugstores and pharmacies.

It is estimated that there are between 750,000 and 800,000

chemists dotted across the length and breadth of our vast nation. Besides medicines, these 'friendly neighbourhood corner stores' sell a variety of other products that a consumer needs. Their tag line should correctly be 'we also sell medicines'.

According to a study by McKinsey in June 2013, the size of the Indian pharmaceutical retail market which was estimated at over ₹43,000 crore (US$ 9.5 billion) in 2006, up from approximately ₹13,000 crore (US$ 3.0 billion) in 1992, was expected to grow to US$ 45 billion by 2020. In addition, chemists in India, like in most pharmacies around the world, sell at least an equivalent amount of FMCG products which are retailed from these shops, bringing the current total share of the retail chemist market to over ₹100,000 crore (US$ 20 billion). A majority of these stores are the traditional 'mom and pop' type. The concept of chain pharmacy stores has just started to evolve in India over the past decade.

As a developing nation opens up its economy, the first sector to give up market share to the private players are the utilities, comprising telecom, power and infrastructure. As the process of liberalization continues, public-sector privatization starts to take place and the private sector starts to take over market share from the public sector. The final stage in any liberalization process is when the organized players come in and take market share from the unorganized sector. This last stage is always sensitive for any democratic government, even though they may recognize the benefits that organized retail chains will give customers and the better purchase prices these chains will be able to offer the primary producers, whether farmers or small-scale manufacturers. However, the large numbers of unorganized players represent a significant vote bank, which any government would naturally be wary of taking head-on.

As I started to study the pharmacy numbers, the vast opportunity sitting in the pharmacy retail space struck me. The segment was growing at over 18 per cent per year and was completely in the unorganized space. This offered some exciting opportunities on the one hand, but on the other, it also demanded a paradigm change in the way medicines were sold and business was done in the well-established business channel of selling medicines.

I remember spending many days observing the buying behaviour of customers and the selling behaviour of the counter staff at various chemists. I observed the physical conditions of a number of them in our country. I also looked at the hygiene levels in these shops, especially since they were selling medicines.

Most chemists in India are small, dusty stores where the customer has to stand outside the shop at the counter. While they sell medicines to cure patients, they are completely unhygienic in their own practices. Standing outside several chemist shops and observing customers' buying behaviour gave me far more insight than I could have gleaned through extensive research.

I observed the following when a customer would go to a chemist store to buy medicines:

- The customer would walk up to the counter and ask for a bottle of cough syrup.
- The chemist would rummage through dusty store shelves and pull out a dusty bottle.
- The chemist would then reach for a dirty rag from underneath the counter and wipe the bottle of cough syrup with this.
- Once the bottle had been cleaned, he would take a paper

bag made out of old newspapers or a plastic bag from a shelf below the counter.
- He would then either blow into the paper bag to open it or wet his thumb and index finger with his spit to open the top of the plastic bag.
- The bottle of cough syrup would then be put into this bag and handed over to the customer.
- If the customer asked for an invoice, it would be issued manually. If no invoice was asked for, it would not be given.
- There would be no checking of the expiry date, the batch number and the maximum retail price printed on the bottle.

Every stage of this purchase process was unhygienic and lacked transparency. Cleaning a bottle with a dirty rag or blowing into a paper bag or putting spit on a plastic bag is unacceptable when selling medicines, and yet the Indian customer did not seem to care. Not taking a bill for a purchase means that if there is a problem with the medicine, there is no way to establish that the medicine has been purchased from that particular chemist.

In the rural areas, I found that the customer had no choice at all. Most medicines were directly dispensed by the chemist based on the patient's symptoms. Customers would simply ask for medicine for a stomach ache or a fever or a headache or something else. The chemist would give one or two tablets to him or her. He would offer an additional service by providing a glass of water from a container lying next to him on a counter, so the customer could gulp the tablet there and then. There was no discussion on the name of the medicine, and since the chemist was dispensing loose tablets, he could charge anything he wanted.

In addition, both in urban and rural India, the availability of medicines at the stores was poor and the issue of the customer having to stand at the counter, whatever the weather, needed to be addressed.

I decided to enter the pharmacy space because of the belief that the unorganized sector would present a big opportunity for growth for any player who could improve on the customer experience, even marginally. There was virtually no organized player present in the market and quite clearly this was a space where I felt I could make a significant difference. In order to do so, it became necessary to ensure that customers found the right ambience, levels of cleanliness, availability of all medicines and reliability of these medicines at Guardian stores.

I was reminded of an old line that I had heard, 'Vision without action is a daydream. Action without a vision is a disaster.'

The Myth of Fake and Spurious Medicines

The pharmaceutical industry was and continues to be faced with a huge issue of 'spurious' medicines and in spite of widespread media coverage, customers generally say that while they are aware of the seriousness of this problem, they are convinced that 'their chemist' cannot sell fake goods.

When I started Guardian Pharmacy, the then health minister, Sushma Swaraj, tried to get a bill passed in Parliament legislating that death penalty should be imposed on manufacturers, distributors and retailers of fake medicines. This legislation, unfortunately, did not go through. I wish it had been passed, since that way old established practices in the pharmaceutical manufacturing, distribution and retail sector would have been broken very quickly.

This is the only industry I have worked in where the

manufacturer/brand owner does not treat the person who pays for his product as his customer, but the person who prescribes the product as his primary customer and the person who sells it as his secondary customer. Most pharmaceutical manufacturers spend all their marketing money on promotions directed at doctors—this trend is now beginning to change through strong implementation of existing laws.

Often when I speak at conferences, in order to communicate the issues relating to fake and spurious medicines, I ask the audience, 'Remember last Sunday when you ate one extra stuffed parantha and this resulted in acidity?'

I see a lot of heads nodding. Then I ask them, 'Then you took two antacid tablets and nothing happened?'

I see more heads nodding. I ask them further, 'When nothing happened, you took two more tablets and still no result, after which you wondered if there is something wrong with you.'

Now I have their complete uninterrupted attention.

Then I tell them the problem: the antacid tablet that they had taken was chalk and nothing else, which is why it had no impact on the acidity.

I have seen innumerable instances of mineral water in injections and haldi powder in multivitamin capsules. Counterfeit medicine manufacturers, distributors and retailers are the bane of society in every country and the strongest possible action should be taken against them. The laws in India are very lax and their implementation leaves much to be desired.

The motive for these manufacturers, distributors and retailers is simply profit and nothing else. They will sell you fake but harmless medicines; they will never sell medicines that will harm you. They will never kill or harm the patient who is their golden goose.

Research Is Important, but Can Delay Startups

I have sat on the boards of many companies and institutions. Whenever we have been confronted by the need to take a quick decision and the board is not ready to take it, we have asked the management teams to conduct research to get more information.

How many times, as boards members of large corporations, have we asked the finance people to run some more numbers or do some more analysis? How many times have we asked the product design people to redo some pack designs because the 'red is not red enough' or the 'green could be a little more green'? How many times have we asked our marketing people to redesign a campaign because we did not think this was 'communicating' the right message for the product?

All this additional information was generally called for because as members of a board, charged with the responsibility of setting direction for the company, we were not ready to take a decision.

For a startup, research is important to set the direction the company wishes to pursue, not to delay decision-making. Research must be an aide to reinforce one's views, not a crutch to say 'I told you so' later, more so if the decision taken does not work out the way it was intended to. At the same time, moving forward purely on impulse may also prove to be expensive.

Nothing is more important for an entrepreneur than to 'put his money where his mouth is'.

Research helps mature companies to fine-tune decision-making. While I am not advocating starting any business enterprise without doing any research, I do believe that too much research delays decisions and, therefore, the startup journey of any new entrepreneur.

I am reminded of a quote of Sir John Harvey Jones, 'Planning is an unnatural process; it is much more fun to do something. The nicest thing about not planning is that failure comes as a complete surprise, rather than being preceded by a period of worry and depression.'

WRITE A CREDIBLE BUSINESS PLAN THAT YOU BELIEVE IN

Trying to predict the future is like trying to drive down a country road at night with no lights while looking out the back window.

—Peter Drucker, Management guru

'Build Boots in India.'

This was the first line I wrote on the first page of my first business plan, as I sat down in 2003 to conceptualize what I wanted to do. These words outlined the boundaries that I wished to work within and I have not wavered in this thinking or crossed these boundaries from the first day. Even before I started working on the business plan, I wrote out the mission statement for the company, which would serve as our guiding principle.

Mission Statement

Guardian's mission is to offer our customers the best and most reliable pharmacy in India and create a modern health-care retail organization, built upon honesty, trust and commitment, using contemporary technology.

As a friendly neighbourhood pharmacy, we will integrate with the community we serve and treat our customers with respect and dignity. We will always abide by the law and will act as responsible corporate citizens.

As we expand our stores, we will aim to provide excellent career opportunities in a fast-growing environment to a diverse group of men and women. We will support these efforts with innovative thinking and training.

The success we achieve will allow us to reinvest in our future and build long-term financial security for our employees and shareholders.

Plan for the Future, Not for Tomorrow

As I started writing, I realized how difficult it was to put pen to paper and to articulate one's thoughts clearly and cogently. The best business plans are written when an entrepreneur writes the plan himself, because that is when the true dreams of the entrepreneur are articulated. If an entrepreneur does not write out his own business plan but relies on someone else to put it together, as indeed I have seen people do, the plan may have inaccuracies and may be developed with a different perspective.

Writing out a detailed business plan and getting it funded properly is the key to making any business successful. Unless the entrepreneur does so, a startup company could be playing 'Russian Roulette', not knowing which chamber the bullet is sitting in!

I have, over the last few years, become a great admirer of Boots and other major chains such as Walgreens and CVS, and have spent many hours walking through the aisles in their stores in the US and UK, observing them and learning from their staff. More recently, Nepstar Pharmacy is showing the way to rapid growth in China. They have built over 2,500 pharmacy stores in the last fifteen years. As explained earlier, I have also spent hundreds of hours observing the chemists in India.

Numbers and assumptions could go wrong once the actual operations of the company start because there could be many variables that are learnt on the job. However, the first business plan helps in defining the parameters and assists the entrepreneur in understanding the areas where his calculation was incorrect or where his assumptions have changed.

While I did write out a complete business plan and prepare my financial spreadsheets, I did not realize, early in the life of Guardian, that retail was a very capital-intensive business proposition and therefore I had to work much harder to keep raising funds for the chain which, in a few years, had started to acquire a life of its own.

Funding is possibly the most difficult part of building a new company. Without sufficient funds in place, it is not advisable to embark upon any entrepreneurial journey. How much is 'sufficient' is a pure judgment call of the entrepreneur, and depends on the business plan that he expects to achieve.

Guardian was started when I had sufficient money of my own to build at least ten stores, so that I would be able to test and prove the concept of organized retail pharmacies.

Getting a mix of debt and equity is important, but every startup business is faced with slower than planned growth and hence debt, and therefore interest, is a cost that is best avoided in the early days.

The Pharmacy Landscape in India

Five years ago as the Indian retail landscape was being explored, every major retail chain took a decision to launch their own pharmacy chain inside their supermarkets.

Within a few months, we had home-grown pharmacies

in Big Bazaar (Tulsi), Reliance Retail (Reliance Wellness), Subhiksha, More, Vishal Mega Mart, Dabur (NewU), Cadila (Dialforhealth) and Religare. In addition, there were over twenty other individuals or companies such as CRS, 98.4, Health & Glow, Likefen, 24 × 7, Trust Chemists, Viva, Rx and some more, which had started their own pharmacy chains. The biggest of them all was Apollo Pharmacy.

While Subhiksha and MedPlus took the discount route, where they gave a flat 10 per cent off on all medicines, others such as Guardian, 98.4 and CRS made reliability their priority. The larger supermarket stores did not have any specific positioning—they were simply trying to add one more 'vertical' inside their large-format stores. Every retail format assumed that if they built a pharmacy inside their large-format stores, consumers would come running to buy their medicines and get their cash registers ringing.

The major global pharmacy retail players are Walgreens (USA), CVS (USA), Rite Aid (USA), Duane Reade (USA), Boots (UK), Shoppers Drug Mart (Canada), Watsons (Hong Kong) and China Nepstar. These chains started selling medicines and have grown over the past few decades, and are now beginning to diversify their products and step into the domain of the supermarkets, which may not necessarily work as well as their traditional business.

When I started the process of raising funds from private equity firms, I was always asked one question by every private equity investor we met: 'How do you think you will be able to survive with so many big players coming into this business?' My response to all them was straightforward and simple: 'I am a great believer in global conventional wisdom. Show me one supermarket chain in the world that has its own pharmacy chain that dominates the business; there is none. Similarly, there is no hospital chain in the world that runs its own pharmacy retail chain. Therefore, why should the assumptions be any different in India and why should the Indian consumer be any different from any other consumer in any other market in the world?'

I don't think any of them ever believed me. It was assumed that if you throw big money into any project, it was bound to succeed. Today, there are only four major pharmaceutical chains left in the country: Apollo, Guardian, Religare and MedPlus. In addition, there are less than six small chains spread across different cities and states like Trust Chemists in Karnataka, GNRC in Guwahati, Planet Health in Ahmedabad, Frank Ross in Kolkata, and Viva and 98.4 in New Delhi. All these pharmacy chains started off as regional players and today some of them, including Guardian, are slowly beginning to expand their presence across the country. I believe that it is better to be a strong regional player than a weak national player.

No one believed me then, but when I meet a lot of these people today, all of them agree with my comments and are now willing to back me completely. As I look at the company today, I can see how much more money will go into building Guardian into a nationwide chain of pharmacies. My primary job will be to keep raising more and more money till the chain generates enough cash to start funding its own expansion.

Plan for Losses

Every new business will lose money. This has to be taken as a 'given'. Making a planned loss is never a problem. Making an unplanned loss and then having to try and justify it is.

Most entrepreneurs, including me, tend to look only at the rosy picture without recognizing the problems that will be faced and without factoring in a number of unplanned costs that will have to be incurred. In spite of the company growing by over 70 per cent compound annual growth rate, we were always on the back foot with our board of directors because we had not met our over-aggressive business plans. No amount of growth over previous years is relevant if we did not meet the budget of the current year. This was always a cause of frustration at most board reviews for the management team of the company.

It is important for every entrepreneur to understand that making money is not easy. Don't believe for a second that revenues will instantly start coming in and customers will flock to your stores. The reality is way different, and you'll fare much better if you understand this and plan for it beforehand, rather than be surprised later.

It is better to plan for losses and state this in your business plan. When monthly reviews are held with the board of directors, it always works to explain how you have overachieved your numbers, rather than keeping high targets and having to explain negative variances each month.

While Guardian kept growing, we were usually behind our self-imposed budgets and therefore we were always pulled up at all our board meetings. After six years of growing at a 'crazy' pace and yet not meeting our budgets, I learned that it is easier to 'under-promise and over-deliver' rather than 'over-promise and under-deliver'.

We have now started including an element of sensitivity into our business, since most businesses do not necessarily achieve what they set out to when they wrote their business plan. This was something that I had learned and always implemented in my many years in the corporate sector, but failed to implement as an entrepreneur.

'Burn' Money—Yes, You Will

No one likes to lose money, and yet it is a well-recognized fact that most new businesses will do so. Some businesses will incur losses for longer periods than others because of their nature. Retail businesses have very long gestation periods. There is nothing to be ashamed of if your business is losing money, as long as you can see the light at the end of tunnel.

I define 'burn' as the amount of money that is committed to be spent each month, irrespective of whether or not the business is generating any cash flow. This is also the amount that needs to be put in every month to meet the cash losses of the company. These expenses are for basic necessities, such as salaries, rentals, utilities and communication costs, as well as for expenses of a capital nature, such as building more stores and fixed assets.

All businesses will burn money and it is necessary to have sufficient funds in the bank to meet the burn. At Guardian, we generally planned for our losses and understood what our monthly burn was likely to be, so that at no stage did we run out of funds. However, we also made lots of errors and were confronted with several unplanned costs, which threw our entire cash planning out of gear and made me scramble to raise additional funds.

RAISE ADEQUATE FUNDING

*So we went to Atari and said, 'Hey, we've got this amazing
thing, even built with some of your parts, and what do you
think about funding us? Or we'll give it to you. We just want
to do it. Pay our salary; we'll come work for you.'
And they said, 'No'. So then we went to Hewlett-Packard,
and they said, 'Hey, we don't need you. You haven't got
through college yet.'*

—Steve Jobs

Every entrepreneur who has a dream believes that raising
money should not be a problem. However I have seen
that getting adequate money to sustain a project is possibly
the single-most important challenge faced by any entrepreneur.

A startup entrepreneur should try and keep sufficient funds
to meet at least twelve months of projected burn. Without
this, the stress on the entrepreneur is very intense and meeting
planned business losses becomes a huge challenge.

Equity from Family

The safest way to build any business is with your own funds,
but these are finite and not sufficient if your dream is bigger
than your savings. I had earned and saved money in my
professional life. Before I started out on my own, I set aside
some money which I call 'drop dead' funds. This, I believed,

would be sufficient for Vera to maintain her standard of living if something were to happen to me. In addition, we lived in a house whose loans had been paid, and I believed I had provided enough for both my sons. The balance of my savings, I decided, would be invested in Guardian.

After investing all my surplus funds, I first turned to my family members for more investment. Vera put in some of her savings, followed by both my sons, who invested ₹1 lakh each, money they had saved from the birthday gifts given by their grandparents.

Both my brothers, Atul and Kapil, also put in some amount. My late sister-in-law Parul called me one day from Singapore and said, 'Bhaiya, I have ₹125,000 saved out of my own income as a teacher and I want to invest this in your dream.'

Support from my family in this journey has been nothing short of extraordinary and I am blessed to have them. Nothing shows more commitment in a business enterprise than a family investing its own money in it.

Equity from Friends

Once my family had put in the money they wanted to, I turned to my friends, and a number of them also decided to invest in my dream.

As the chain started to grow, more friends, former colleagues and friends of friends started to contact me to invest in it. We had to quickly set up systems to manage the funds. A lot of time was spent in preparing presentations to share with these investors.

As the company kept expanding, more and more individuals expressed a strong interest in investing their money. Today, Guardian has over forty-five investors and I am grateful to each one of them for the trust and confidence they have reposed in me and my colleagues. While they have not got any returns on their investment so far, I am sure they will be able to get substantial returns when we list the company.

Raising money from friends of friends, people whom you have never met, can become a challenge. While I have a moral commitment on the investment by my friend's friend, this person looks at the investment differently. For such an investor, return in a finite period of time is the only reason for investing in my business. He did so because he felt that I was a credible businessman. I have faced a few shareholders who actually asked me to refund their equity after their share certificates had been issued, knowing fully well that under the law this cannot be done.

It is always good to sign an agreement with each shareholder so that there are no differences later, and it is important for the entrepreneur to ensure that he gets the appropriate rights to keep the business moving. Matters such as 'tag along rights' and 'drag along rights' are best discussed and agreed upon at the time of signing the shareholders' agreement, rather than being left as open issues for discussions and debate at a later date.

Debt

If an entrepreneur keeps taking more and more equity, his stake in his own business gets reduced or 'diluted' as more shareholders come into the business. Therefore, all businesses need debt to grow and to prevent a high degree of dilution for the entrepreneur.

However, startups face the big dilemma of how to raise debt. As a professional manager, I was often told by my banker friends that all bankers were looking for good entrepreneurs and good projects to invest in. Once I started approaching them for loans to build Guardian, everyone asked for 'collateral' to secure the debt. Putting the application in the required format of the bank is itself a huge challenge for a new businessman. I had to ask a consultant, who was recommended to me by a banker, for assistance to complete the application.

Doing the rounds of banks and explaining my 'proposal' was a big challenge, and time frames that were important for me never seemed to match those of the 'friendly' banker. I was fortunate enough to meet a group of bankers from Syndicate Bank's corporate finance branch in New Delhi, who 'adopted' me and decided to process Guardian's working capital and term loan papers quickly.

However, they too, like all other bankers, wanted a collateral asset before they could sanction a loan. When I asked them how professional managers like me would be able to put up an immovable asset as collateral, they said that they understood my position, but their hands were tied and they would not be able to recommend a loan to their 'higher authorities'.

I realized after several rounds of meetings and intensive discussions that all the talk of 'intellectual capital' and 'good promoters' meant very little to a banker whose simple credo was, 'It does not matter what your education is, what your professional track record is or how strong your project is. Get an immovable asset as collateral, give your unlimited and unconditional personal guarantees and take a loan.'

After much thought and deliberation, I decided to give them our house as collateral for the working capital and term loan facilities. The value of the house was four times that of the loan. Giving our house as collateral was not a smart move, and I have faced many anxious moments whenever I thought about the consequences of not being able to repay the loan in time. As an entrepreneur, it is never a wise decision to give your personal home as collateral, but I was faced with tough choices and had no other option.

In addition to taking my house as the collateral, the bankers also insisted on taking my personal guarantee to further securitize their loan! Bankers are supposed to assess projects and take risks to maximize returns for their shareholders. Nationalized banks are also supposed to promote entrepreneurship for the growth of the nation. This experience of raising money from Syndicate Bank left me wondering whether our banking system was designed to support entrepreneurs or simply to give money to well-established and profitable companies.

Yet, when we later raised large sums of private equity, the same bank insisted that we place these liquid funds with them at low interest rates. They kept reminding me of the long business association between Guardian and the bank, as well as my 'moral' obligation to the bank that had supported me in my time of need. How does this make our modern banking system, which is supposed to have lofty ideals of building the nation, any different from the age-old moneylender, who kept your land and your jewellery along with your moral commitment before he gave you any loans?

Raising early debt was probably the hardest part of building Guardian. I realized that twenty-five years of experience and credibility had no 'bankable' value. I also recognized that I had the ability to build a business, but not to raise bank loans. I needed to either learn how to raise funds or get expert advice on raising borrowed funds.

Immediately on receipt of our private equity funds, I repaid all the debt and released my house from the bank. The promoter of any business must ensure that his house must never be put in jeopardy, no matter how strong the business model or how confident the promoter may be about his dream. I have also understood in my journey that if a personal guarantee must be given, the promoter must never include the spouse as a guarantor.

Working Capital

Retail companies need quite a bit of working capital, since we have a lot of stocks and inventory. While established retail companies in the world tend to work with 'negative' working capital (which really means that they have mastered the art of using their suppliers' funds to pay for their stocks), new companies like Guardian need to invest in stocks.

Like debt, raising working capital is a challenge for most new businesses and similar collaterals are always asked for by the 'friendly' bankers; this despite the fact that inventory is normally deemed to be a liquid asset and considered an excellent collateral for well-established and profitable businesses. We have struggled to explain to bankers the value of our pharmaceutical products' inventory and how easy it is for them to treat this as collateral for working capital funding. Banks refused to accept that pharmaceutical distributors are obligated to take back all expired and slow-moving products within the agreed time periods. We showed them agreements that were applicable to the entire industry, but were not able to convince the risk managers in these banks.

Most banks still feel happier with a fixed asset that they can take as collateral. This once again brings us back to the problem of plenty. Companies that don't need funds have banks chasing them and organizations that need money are chasing the banks.

Everyone seems to be caught in this vicious circle.

Private Equity

Raising private equity will always dilute the shareholding of the promoter of the company. At conferences I have often been asked to share my views on the impact of dilution of the promoters' stake when private equity is brought in.

It is my belief that once a company is established, the promoters' priority has to change completely—from guarding and enhancing one's own wealth to ensuring the growth of the company, which now has many more stakeholders including employees, creditors, vendors, governments and, most importantly, the customers.

At an appropriate stage in the life of a business, it is necessary to raise private equity for the company to ensure that its growth does not suffer. The old adage is that it is better to have 25 per cent of one thousand than to have 100 per cent of one hundred. Only when a company grows will its value grow and with it, the value of its shareholders' wealth.

In the long run, fighting dilution will prove detrimental to the future of the entrepreneur's dream.

A number of entrepreneurs mistakenly believe that they can handle fundraising on their own because someone in their family or in their friends' circle has had experience of raising money. In several cases I have met entrepreneurs who want to raise additional funds to grow their business, but are not willing to pay any fees to an investment banker to help them do so.

Investors prefer to deal through an intermediary who has a reputation to protect in the industry and therefore will be expected to be 'honest' in his dealings. In addition, potential investors can ask tough questions to the management through the middleman. Such intermediaries are generally investment bankers, whose primary role is get investors and investees together and help both parties to understand each other's aspirations and concerns.

Two years after starting Guardian, when I started to expand my business aggressively and needed to inject additional funding, I engaged a boutique investment banking firm based in Mumbai.

The first step, to create an information memorandum, was really an articulation of my dreams. But soon I learned that it is better to make a conservative first information memorandum and get potential investors to buy in on this, rather than make aggressive projections to start with.

I met numerous private equity fund investors over a period of one year. In all our meetings, the investors invariably had a similar set of questions.

I was fortunate to get a strong private equity partner, who believed in my dream. Not only did they give us money to grow the business, they also worked very closely with the Guardian management team to review our business plans and strategies. They invested twice in the company in a span of twenty-four months, showing their faith in the business. Over the past five years we have brought in a second strong private equity player to bolster the funds available in the company for future growth.

Unless your private equity partner shares your dream, there will be contrary positions between them and you at most board meetings, which will prove dysfunctional for the business. It is also important for both partners to agree on the time horizon for the exit of the private equity investor. I have seen a lot of companies being pushed into going for an Initial Public Offering (IPO) very early in their lives, even though the promoter felt that the timing was not right.

KNOW YOUR CUSTOMERS

A customer is the most important visitor on our premises. He is not dependent on us. We are dependent on him. He is not an interruption in our work. He is the purpose of it. He is not an outsider in our business. He is part of it. We are not doing him a favour by serving him. He is doing us a favour by giving us an opportunity to do so.

—Anonymous

A pharmacy is the only business I have ever worked in where, theoretically, every single person is a potential customer. Our customers are very simply segmented into men, women, children and senior citizens.

Some doctors prescribe the most expensive antibiotics to patients when the same salt is available in a generic medicine for less than 5 per cent of the cost. When I asked some of these doctors what makes them prescribe such expensive medicines when cheaper alternatives exist, they simply said, 'If we don't prescribe the most expensive medicine, our patient thinks that the treatment we have recommended is not good enough.'

I have always been surprised by this—linking getting well to the price of a tablet certainly seems a little far-fetched. On the other hand, I have seen doctors prescribing generic medicines in rural India where their prescription is linked to the cost of the medicine and the patient's ability to afford it. This has often made me wonder what is it that makes a patient well—the medicine or the cost of the medicine?

A pharmacy is the only retail format which has a conversion ratio in excess of 85 per cent. This means that more than 85 per cent of customers who walk into a pharmacy normally buy something. Customers normally do not go into a pharmacy simply to 'browse'. I monitor the conversion ratio in a store very carefully and if the conversion ratio drops, alarm bells go off. Either the store is poorly stocked, in which case we are losing sales, or there is an issue with the sales staff, leading to poor customer service. This has to be handled quickly.

Understanding our consumer was a big challenge for all of us at Guardian. While I used to spend several hours in our stores talking to customers, given the richness of India's demography, I was always faced with a huge challenge in trying to understand the unique needs of each customer.

In the initial years, we did not have the resources to conduct expensive market surveys. But in the last few years, we have started to conduct research to understand the profile of our customer, as well as to understand how the consumer perceives the Guardian brand.

The Indian Pharmacy Customer and What a Customer Expects

Based on extensive market research, we have found that the top five drivers for a customer at a pharmacy are:

Location: Customers want easy access to their pharmacy. They don't like to spend too much time in parking or paying for parking. Customers also prefer to buy medicines from stores that are close to their home; stores close to their place of work come a distant second.

Sales assistance: Pharmacists are generally the first point of contact for a customer when they wish to understand which medicines have been prescribed by their doctor, as well as to understand the side effects of these medicines, if any. I have often seen our customers asking our pharmacists to explain what a particular medicine is for or to explain the side effects of another medicine.

Availability of products: The general experience of most customers is that their chemist is not able to provide them with all the medicines that they need when they visit the store. Given the large number of medicines that doctors have to choose from when they write a prescription, as well as the equally large number of new brands and new medicines being developed and aggressively marketed by the pharmaceutical companies, ensuring 100 per cent availability will always be a big challenge for any pharmacy.

At Guardian, we do try and ensure that we provide as many medicines as possible and home-deliver medicines that are not available in the store.

Trust: The problem of fake medicines is rampant in our country and most customers are beginning to recognize this because of the good work done by the Government of India. Customers now look at expiry dates more closely and ask for a printed bill. However, the myth of someone else facing the problem still remains.

Ease and speed of billing: When a customer walks into a pharmacy, he wants to get his medicines quickly and leave as soon as possible. He is generally not willing to wait or browse. While this is a normal behaviour for any consumer at a chemist's, the expectation of a quick turnaround has been enhanced because most chemist shops in our country are counter stores and do not give customers an opportunity to browse and look at other products while he is waiting for his prescription to be filled.

The Indian Pharmacy Customer

Customers in India are as demanding as anywhere else in the world, but they are willing to listen to the retailers' point of view as well, especially if the sales assistant is well trained and his or her knowledge and understanding of the products seems credible.

Tolerant: I have found customers to be generally very tolerant in our country. If the sales staff in our stores make a mistake, the customers are willing to listen to our side of the story with a sympathetic ear. Very often, I have seen a customer stand up for an errant sales staff when his supervisor has pulled him up in an attempt to improve service levels.

It is generally believed that most customers give a store three opportunities. If they meet with disappointment of any kind more than three times, it is unlikely they will come back to shop at the store in a hurry. Given the fact that most stores repeatedly disappoint customers, we at Guardian have been fortunate to have had many more opportunities from our customers. I realize that if a customer walks away from Guardian because he is disappointed with our service levels, he comes back not because he wants to but because the other stores in the neighbourhood have been equally disappointing.

We have been working very hard to try and meet the expectations of our consumers and I can see the light at the end of our 'training' tunnel. I am confident that our customers will continue to see a significant improvement in our service levels.

Price conscious: The Indian consumer is known to be very price conscious. Discounts, promotions, markdowns and other value-based offers are always picked up very quickly. It is important to differentiate between the Indian consumers' desire for 'value for money' as compared to 'cheap products of poor quality'. The price of the products has to be right but the quality must not be compromised.

Delay in billing: I have seen customers wait patiently as they watch store staff 'fill their prescriptions' or take out their medicines from boxes behind the counter. But the moment the medicines have been taken out, the customer is not willing to wait for more than thirty seconds to get the bill, pay and leave. This becomes difficult, especially if there are several customers in the store. This delay is possibly the most frequent complaint I receive from customers.

In order to handle this, we normally add additional billing points. We have also created a small ledge beneath the counter in our busy stores where the medicines can be taken out in small plastic baskets and kept out of view of the customer. Complaints for billing delays dropped sharply immediately after we took this step.

At the same time, we have trained our customer-care executives to walk up to a 'waiting' customer, engage him in a dialogue and talk to him about promotional offers of Guardian brands and other products. While waiting, a customer is very receptive to striking up a conversation with the store staff. We found that this way our average bill size started to increase, since the customers started to buy a lot of other items while they were waiting.

Discounts: The Indian customer, like any other, loves to get a discount, no matter how large or small. But the margin structure on medicines does not warrant any discounting at all. However, discounts on medicines are generally given by smaller chemist shops or on high-margin medicines, like the drugs needed for oncology patients, as a result of which most customers have started to expect a discount. This practice of asking for discounts is more prevalent in the older and more densely populated parts of a city. Customers located in newer areas don't seem to do so.

At Guardian we generally do not offer a discount on medicines. The only exception we have made is at our hospital stores in Uttar Pradesh, where we have agreed with the state government to pass on a part of our margins to the patients to reduce their expenditure on medicines. In addition, we have launched a discount scheme for senior citizens at our retail stores where we offer up to 10 per cent discount.

Finally, we offer a discount in the form of Guardian XtraValu loyalty points on all purchases. Customers are able to redeem these points to buy any of the nominated products under this scheme in our stores.

Non-availability: New medicines are being launched every day and medical representatives of the pharmaceutical companies are in constant dialogues with doctors encouraging them to prescribe their products. At some of our stores, we have encountered doctors who prescribe medicines from one company every Monday and Thursday, another company every Tuesday and Friday and a third company every Wednesday and Saturday. Given the large numbers of SKUs a pharmacy normally stocks and the huge number of brands and generics of the same salt that are required to be kept, ensuring 100 per cent availability of the medicines in every prescription becomes a challenge.

When a customer walks into a pharmacy and hands over his prescription, the standard practice is that the chemist places the prescription on his counter top and then tells the customer what is not available. More often than not, the customer takes back the prescription and walks over to the next store in the same market. In order to tackle this problem, I asked our pharmacists to keep the prescription in their hand and not on the counter. They would then tell the customer which medicines were available at the time in the store, and offer to home-deliver the remaining ones in an hour

The customer would not be able to grab the prescription and walk out of the store to our competitor. The moment we implemented this plan, our prescription conversions increased substantially and we had many more satisfied customers. I found that custody of the prescription was key to making the sale.

What Upsets a Customer?

While most customers are willing to tolerate reasonable levels of inefficiencies and errors, the old adage comes into play: 'To err is human but if the eraser wears out ahead of the pencil, you are overdoing it!'

I have noticed that some of the common reasons that irritate customers are:

Not meeting commitments: There have been a number of instances where our store staff made a commitment to deliver a product to a customer within an agreed time period. As long as this commitment was kept, we knew we had a happy customer. But if the commitment was not honoured, then the customer would be unhappy. If at that time the store staff attempted to give a 'smart' answer then the customer was in his right to get upset.

Poor service: I have experienced poor service quite often in various stores, including our own. When I want to buy a pair of shoes and ask for a size nine and a half, the store assistant tries to push a size nine because he does not have my size. When I question this, his response normally is 'When you start using the shoe it will open up and fit your foot much better.'

At Guardian too, like most chemists, we have had to stop the practice of handing over a strip of ten milligram tablets when a customer asks for five milligram ones, and asking the customer to take half of the former. This is not right, since the pharmacology of the tablet changes when we take half a tablet. If it were so simple, pharmaceutical companies would only manufacture one size and ask patients to take half or one quarter of the tablet to meet their required dosage.

Arrogance: As I have stated elsewhere, there is no place for one's ego in a retail store. If a store staff member is arrogant the customer picks up such body language very quickly.

Passing the buck: Store staff often tell a customer that certain goods are not available because despite repeated requests, the head office is not sending these products to them. In some cases, I have seen the store staff dial the phone number of the supply chain head and hand over the phone to the angry customer. This does not go down well. Any member of store staff must never pass the buck to his head office in an attempt to save his own skin since this weakens the perceptions of the customer about the brand. Internal issues of a company must be addressed internally.

Questioning a customer's intelligence: I am sure a lot of us have experienced a situation where we go to a restaurant and ask for a glass of cold water. When the water arrives and we don't find it to be cold, we tell the waiter to change it. How often have we seen a waiter touch the glass and then tell the customer that in his view, the water is cold enough?

This is a classic example of a staff member questioning a customer's intelligence. Anyone in the retail business has to accept a customer's viewpoint as long as the customer is reasonable.

Arguing with a customer: This is a cardinal sin in the retail business. Arguing with a customer may enable a store staff member to win a small battle but in the long run, he would not only have lost the sale but the customer.

Customer Complaints

Whenever any customer takes the trouble to write in to us to lodge a complaint, I believe he deserves an immediate response. All customer complaints come directly to me and I attempt to answer each one of them personally. I nominate one of my colleagues to address the complaint and then follow up later to ensure that the matter has been addressed to the satisfaction of the customer.

I have received several follow-up letters from our customers once their complaints have been addressed, and I know that these people have now become our brand ambassadors. A customer whose complaint has been addressed will always make it a point to share his experience with other friends and family members.

It has been my long-standing belief that only the customers who care for Guardian take the trouble to complain.

'One More Sale'

There are only two ways to increase the sale in a retail store—first, to increase the number of customers who visit the store and second, to increase the amount of money each customer spends there. Both variables are challenging and while we invested in our brand to build our credibility, in the hope that people would flock to our stores, we also used various promotions to encourage them to spend more.

I once asked my store staff to try and sell one additional item to every customer, irrespective of what they sold or how much it cost. 'One More Sale' became our screen saver at all stores to constantly remind them of this. With over twenty thousand customers a day, if we could get each of them to spend even an additional ₹10 at the store, the revenue of the company would increase by over ₹7 crore a year.

My primary objective in implementing 'One More Sale' was to get our store staff to start talking to our customers. Once they had gotten over their initial shyness, I found that they were able to convince people to increase their spending quite significantly. In the process, we managed to increase our average revenue per customer as well.

MY FIRST STORE

Nothing splendid has ever been achieved except by those who dared believe that something inside them was superior to circumstance.

—Bruce Barton, author and politician

Opening the first store was the biggest step forward in my entrepreneurial journey, and earning my first rupee as an entrepreneur my biggest challenge.

I wanted to open a small shop somewhere in Gurgaon, on the outskirts of Delhi, to test the soundness of my concept and, more importantly, my ability to make this transition. I had earmarked a monthly rental budget of ₹25,000.

A real-estate broker friend told me about this retail space at a new market called Galleria in DLF Phase IV, Gurgaon, but cautioned that the owner preferred multinational companies. At the meeting with the owner, it became clear that his main concern was my ability to pay him the monthly rental. I gave him thirty-six post-dated monthly cheques and the deal was sealed.

This market was less than one kilometre's distance from my house, one of the main considerations in selecting this location.

My first store was 250 square feet, not on the main road but inside the market square, a location most marketing pandits would believe was not right. The position of this store might not have passed muster if measured against Conrad Hilton's 'location, location, location' philosophy. However, it had an excellent corner location with two sides open. This gave me outstanding branding possibilities. I was very excited when I signed the store lease agreement, but I also realized that every square inch of the store had to be designed well. I had no experience of designing a store, much less running one.

Store Design and Renovation

As I started to think of the first store design, I wanted to ensure that every design decision I took should be scalable to one hundred stores in a few years.

A young designer, Manish Chandra, put together the concept drawings of the first Guardian store. I spent many hours with Manish working on the layout of the interiors, the shelves, the billing counter, the wiring diagram, the telephone cables and the air conditioners. Then came the testing of floor tiles and electrical fixtures. While our tiles and wall colours have remained unchanged, our electrical fixtures have been upgraded since the early days. The strategy of the 'same look and feel' has helped us in creating a chain and a strong pharmacy brand.

Signage and Stationery

Standardization of store signage and stationery is always a challenge for most Indian companies. I have often encountered people from the same company presenting different visiting cards. I'm not a big fan of such a practice and made sure that all the stationery in the company, including business cards for the employees, was standardized. No one had the authority to change the brief given to the printer.

Launch Advertisements

Since our positioning platform was 100 per cent reliability in a country plagued with fake medicines, we decided to tell actual stories of customers who had fought a battle with health issues and won. As a pharmacy, I realized that every person, irrespective of age, sex, caste, creed or financial background, was my potential customer.

Given that we needed models who would work for us for free, we decided to use friends and relatives. We continue to use our store staff as well as spouses of our staff members as models in our advertisements.

We also announced a campaign to publish the stories of all customers who would like to tell us about their struggles, and were inundated with real-life health-related battles.

Pharmacy Licence

Getting a pharmacy licence was not an easy task. Raj Sehgal, our senior manager, marketing, was the first pharmacist whose licence we used and I know how much work he had to do to secure the first licence for the company. The provisions under the Drugs and Cosmetics Act in India are challenging and must be met. Some of the requirements of the licence are:

- Minimum store area must be 110 square feet.
- Minimum height between ceiling and floor must be 9 feet 2 inches.
- Only one door, both for entry and exit, is permitted under the licence, irrespective of the size of the store.
- Ceiling and walls must be made from brick and mortar. Wood or any other material is not allowed.
- A qualified pharmacist's licence, along with his or her

bio-data and other degrees. The original degree of the pharmacist must be kept by the company, since there have been several instances of multiple uses of one degree.

- Copy of rent receipt confirming that the applicant has taken the store on rent.
- Original blueprint of the shop (photocopy of the design is not accepted by the authorities).
- One refrigerator with a minimum capacity of 165 litres. The receipt of purchase of the refrigerator has to be attached to the application form.
- Payment of a fee of ₹3,000 and a copy of the treasury receipt.
- Air conditioning is recommended for all chemist shops, though this requirement is generally not enforced.
- Proof of ownership of the premises by the landlord.

On asking a senior government official in the drug department about the reason why only one entry and exit was permitted despite the size of the store, his response was, 'We have this rule so that you won't run away when we conduct a raid.'

To this day, my larger stores, which are over 3,000 square feet, have only one entrance and exit. So much for fire safety!

The height of the store, or more importantly, the distance between the floor and the ceiling, is always taken as gospel by the drug licensing authorities. No one till date has been able to explain to me why a particular height is important to sell medicines. In a few stores, my colleagues in the project team made a mistake in the measurement of the height and we completed these stores with a height of nine feet or nine feet, one inch. When the drug licensing authority visited these stores, he rejected our licence application because the store was seen to be non-compliant with the drug laws. Since we could not raise the height of the ceiling, we were left with no alternative but to chisel away one inch from the floor, so that the minimum height requirement was met. The moment we lowered the floor, we got our licence.

If you walk into a Guardian store where you actually have to step down a couple of inches to enter the store, you now know the reason why!

Finally, the drug licence is given in the name of the company for a specific pharmacist. If the pharmacist is on leave and the company has not registered another pharmacist, then the store cannot be opened. All organized retail pharmacy chains struggle with this requirement since there is generally high attrition at stores, given the job opportunities with new chains.

Store Ambience

I was keen to open the first store with a different ambience from what consumers had been used to seeing in a traditional chemist shop.

In-store music: I decided that I wanted to have music playing in the background of the store all the time that it was open. Instead of simply playing any music, I consulted a well-known musicologist who put together a CD with a mix of Indian classical, Western classical, piano rendition of popular Hindi film songs and some old English songs. This was a well-thought-through collection, based on store timings and our expectation of customer visits. We decided together that we would have Indian classical in the morning for the first few hours, followed by Western classical in the afternoon. The early evening would switch to popular Hindi movie piano recitals.

Since all store computers had a CD player as a part of the standard hardware, on one of my visits I was surprised to hear loud music coming from one of our stores. When I entered, I found that the store staff had switched off the approved music and changed to loud film music. On another visit to another store, I found three of the staff huddled behind the computer, watching the screen with rapt attention. They did not notice me walking in so I went behind them to look at what had caught their attention so much that they had not even noticed a potential customer. I was horrified to find that the store staff was watching a pornographic CD in the middle of the day. We were fortunate that it was me and not a customer who had walked in at this time. All three of them were dismissed on the spot.

We were thus forced to disable the CD drives as well as all USB ports from all store computers. As a result of staff misuse, we also ended up saving money on redundant hardware, but we had to stop playing music in the stores, which was an inherent part of the brand.

Hot and cold air conditioning: Given the severity of the summers and winters in New Delhi, I installed an air conditioner with heating facility as well. This was done with the objective of providing customers an ambient temperature of 21°C round the year. While the first installation worked, we realized that the cost of air conditioners with cooling and heating was at least 50 per cent greater than a simple non-heating air conditioner. We stopped putting dual-function air conditioners in our stores thereafter. Further, the first few stores had air conditioners with remote controls. Within a few days we found that store staff would lose the remote control and then start switching the air conditioner on and off from the master switch. This was not good for the compressor, but there was no way that we could get them to understand. So we dropped the idea of having remote controls and saved more money in the process.

I was quick to realize the implications of the cost of replication as well as the cost of a mistake when multiplied several times in a chain.

Launch of the First Guardian Store

25 August 2003. This date was a milestone in my journey as an entrepreneur, as it marked the opening of the first Guardian Pharmacy store.

I had returned after dropping my older son Varun in Singapore and was scheduled to leave for Canada with my younger son Ashwin the same week to drop him at Pearson College, Victoria, in Canada. During this gap of a few days and between extensive travelling, I opened the first Guardian store.

We opened the first Guardian store with a staff of three people, one pharmacist, one customer-care executive and one delivery boy. I stood behind the counter myself, waiting nervously for our first customer and within a few minutes of opening the store, I made the first sale.

The first invoice was for a sum of ₹30. Since we were unique in the market in terms of our store design and had used the word 'pharmacy' in our branding, a number of people came and looked at the store from the outside but walked away, not knowing what we were selling. It took people a while to understand that a pharmacy was a chemist shop. When we closed the till at the end of the first day, our opening-day sale was only ₹5,000, but we had filled twenty prescriptions and serviced twenty customers, and all of us were very upbeat on our day's achievements. However, we had also lost another fifteen customers because we did not have their medicines in stock. We made a note to order these drugs.

This started the evolution of a 'shortage register' in Guardian. Each store of ours has a shortage register where the store staff writes down manually what medicines are not available and then sends this in a daily report to the warehouses. This system has now been computerized, though I still believe that manually writing the shortage in a register made the store staff keep a closer track of the inventory.

Guardian had started its operations and we were on our way.

For the first six months, I would start my day at 8 a.m. I did everything from wiping the floors and cleaning every shelf and glass pane to arranging the shop display and throwing out the garbage. I would stand behind the counter and handle customers—generating bills, collecting cash and packing medicines. These six months helped me understand the expectations customers had from their chemist. I would also order the inventory and do the data entry to record stock receipts. This experience of directly running my store gave me an amazing understanding of the business and our customers. No job was too small for me in my own store. I have even carried goods in my car to be delivered to customers.

BRAND NAME, LOGO, TAG LINE AND CORPORATE COLOURS

Your premium brand had better be delivering something special, or it's not going to get the business.

—Warren Buffett

Brand Guardian

It is critical to select a brand name that will convey the correct meaning of the business enterprise, first to the entrepreneur, then to the employees and finally to the customers.

Brands are like children. They need constant supervision and investment to grow and prosper. The care and attention we normally observe when naming a child is no different from that needed in naming a brand. I ran through hundreds of names before I was able to settle on Guardian.

I applied for registration of the Guardian Pharmacy brand name with the Trade Marks Registry, Government of India, but getting the final trademark approval took almost five years. As we started opening stores, I was pleasantly surprised to find a huge acceptance of the brand name among customers.

Getting the company staff to understand the importance of respecting your brand is a huge challenge. I used to find our people misusing company stationery and paper bags, using our Guardian-branded printed material to wrap foodstuff, standing on top of a company poster or damaged signage, and so on.

On one of my rounds when I saw a store personnel standing with his shoes on, on a Guardian-branded point of sale poster, instead of getting upset like I normally would have done, I decided to try something different. I asked him to write his name on a blank sheet of paper in bold capital letters. Once he did this, I placed the paper on the ground and asked him to stand on the paper. His immediate reaction was one of horror: 'Sir, how can you ask me to put my shoes on my name?' I pointed to the Guardian poster under his feet and showed him that his shoes were on the name of his company. The message was loud and clear. This rapidly spread through the company. I have never seen any staff member disrespecting the Guardian brand since.

In a survey conducted by IMRB International, Guardian was seen to have the highest recall as a brand by customers in North India. A strong brand with strong values will survive well beyond the life of its founder or any of the managers of the company. Your brand is created by your customers.

Brand Aushadhi

As we started to expand our operations into semi-urban and rural areas, we found that the word 'Guardian' was too anglicized for people to identify with. At some stores, we noticed that we had used the Guardian brand but then to clarify what we sold, we'd had to add in Hindi the words 'Angrezi Dawaiyan' (Western allopathic medicines, as compared to Ayurveda, Unani and homeopathy). The Hindi line was not fitting in with the overall brand image and we needed to do something completely different.

In order to retain our overall brand proposition of reliability and not deviate from our customer offering, we searched for a name that meant 'medicine' across multiple Indian languages, and decided to use the Sanskrit word 'aushadhi' as our brand name. We used the same font as Guardian, but changed the colour and the treatment we gave to the logo.

Logo

The logo of the company must have a clear identity that embodies the values of the brand as well as encapsulates the vision of the founder. Hence, lot of thought has to go into finalizing the logo. My brief for the Guardian logo was to bring uniqueness to it. I wanted a 'healthy unisex human being' reaching out for the sun. I used the sun as a part of the logo because for Indians, the sun is a source of healing, energy, light and wellness. The sun and the healthy human being were incorporated in a purple cross.

Later, when we developed the logo of our rural pharmacy chain, Aushadhi, I reversed the logo. This time I put half the sun with a family of three (one man, one woman and one child), with a deep saffron-coloured medical cross rising from behind the sun.

Tag Line

The tag line of the company must evolve from the brand name, the logo and the value proposition that the business proposes to offer.

Guardian's value proposition, when we started, was our ability to offer 100 per cent reliability of medicines to our customers. We therefore decided to add '100% Reliable' to our logo and brand name, making these three entities into one composite unalterable single unit. We have used positioning statements such as 'Your Family Chemist'; 'Your Friendly Neighbourhood Pharmacy'; and 'The Chemists India Trusts', but our primary tag line of '100% Reliable' continues unchanged. Many other chains have attempted to copy our tag line with words like 'Genuine Medicines' or '100% Trust' or something similar. This position of reliability has worked well for our brand.

We also translated the '100% Reliable' tag line into Hindi and added a line 'Dawa Sahi Dam Wahi' (Right medicine at the same price). A few weeks after we had run this tag line at our stores, the local drug inspector wanted us to withdraw it since there were complaints that this tag line, by implication, meant that others were selling the wrong medicines. Though I disagreed with the logic of the drug inspector, we withdrew this advertising campaign. For our Aushadhi brand, our tag line was easily translated into Hindi and said '100% Bharosa' or 100 per cent reliable.

Corporate Colours

I have seen some young companies change their logo colours within a few months or years of starting operations and I have seen others not being consistent in their use of colours. The corporate colour has to become a part of the lifestyle of the company.

Over the past few years, the purple colour has started getting identified with Guardian Pharmacy, and I often find a neighbourhood chemist having painted his shutters purple to be able to pass off his store as an affiliate of Guardian.

The colour of the Aushadhi logo is a bright orange–saffron mix, representing the colours of rural India. We created a differentiation between the two brands, both through the logo and the colour, without changing the value proposition of the company, and though we have not yet pushed Aushadhi too much, I know that in the next few years, Aushadhi will become a strong brand of the Guardian family.

BUILDING NEW STORES

*Design is an opportunity to continue telling the story,
not just to sum everything up.*

—Tate Linden, head, Stokefire

Location

Conrad Hilton's famous adage about location holds true for retail stores as well. Customers want their neighbourhood pharmacy to be easily accessible. We have opened stores that have taken off and stores that have not worked. The primary reason for the failure of some shops has been location.

Some examples of the poor locations we chose:

- We opened a store on a busy highway in Gurgaon and I had thought that it would be a runaway success. When we did not see the sales pick up, we did some basic research and realized that customers found it difficult to stop on a busy highway. Even if they did decide to stop, parking was a huge challenge.
- We opened stores inside a number of supermarkets. All pharmacy chains initially assumed that opening a store within a supermarket would work very well. However, this was wrong since most of us had come to this conclusion based on data we had seen from international chains. None

of these stores worked since the customer was not willing to buy medicines inside a supermarket.

- We opened stores inside malls. None of these worked and we realized that when a customer wants to buy medicines, he is not willing to brave heavy traffic, park in the basement of the mall, pay parking charges, and take the elevator or steps, all to access a pharmacy.

- Opening pharmacies outside hospitals is generally considered to be an absolutely safe bet. While we have some excellent locations, we had to shut a few stores because we found that the hospital itself, based on which we were building our business plan, was either poorly located or was many months away from opening.

- We also tried to set up stores inside the booming call centres. I assumed that with a large young population working in these, if we were able to offer convenience of purchasing medicines the store would be very successful. My assumptions were wrong. These youngsters had no interest in buying medicines at their place of work.

- I had thought that opening stores at the newly opened Delhi Metro stations would be a huge success. I took an appointment with E. Sreedharan, the then CEO of Delhi Metro Rail Corporation, and explained to him the value of bringing in a single brand pharmacy at all his stations as service to the commuters. He was very receptive and within a few minutes he gave us permission to open pharmacies at six locations.

These did not work well because some of our stores were located at the entrance to the station and commuters were not allowed to carry shopping into the trains. Other stores were located at the exit and we realized that commuters

were in a hurry to reach home so did not want to stop
and buy medicines at the station.

However, we have built stores at excellent locations as well.
Stores in neighbourhood markets where customers came for
their daily shopping have always worked well for us. These
stores have consistently delivered the highest revenue per square
foot. With the mushrooming of condominiums, we tried a
new format inside the condominium stores. These stores have
been profitable.

I was faced with an interesting dilemma at one stage as we
were rolling out stores rapidly. Whichever location we would
go to, we would find that the landlord had an offer from a
bank to set up an ATM. When we asked for the rental, we
would be given very high rates. I was not able to understand
how banks could afford to pay so much money, or why they
would pay so much above the value of the area, based on the
local market. Similarly, we found that the real estate prices in
Jaipur suddenly shot up one year because the state government
had licensed a large number of liquor vends, and therefore
landlords preferred to rent their stores out to sell alcohol
instead of medicines.

Standard Cookie-Cutter Approach

Since my plan was to build a retail chain that would span
the length and breadth of India, it was important for me
to adopt a 'cookie-cutter' approach to building stores. This
meant that everything we needed to build our stores had to
be easily available and inexpensive. No individual store could
be customized and all the material we used in building them
should be available anywhere in the country. In addition, the

material that we used would necessarily have to be easy to install so that craftsmen and workers of varying skill sets would be able to implement our standards.

Store Design

Standardizing store designs was something I decided to implement from the first store. It was critical to ensure that the 'look and feel' of every store was identical so that customers would feel that the service and reliability they got at one store would be replicated in the others.

We decided to establish standard parameters for every step of the store renovation process. These standards covered the smallest detail including listing out colour and thickness of tiles, colour of the walls and ceiling, exact specifications of wiring, quality of wood to be used, etc. In addition, we laid down three approved suppliers for each item. This helped us to establish our standards and make sure that these are followed to the letter. Any deviation from the standard results in the manager in charge of the development as well as the contractor being severely reprimanded.

In addition, every activity in the process of building a store was timed. We put all this data into a simple chart whereby everyone would know which activities had to done sequentially and what could be started concurrently. Our software also enabled us to track which department was on schedule and which was running behind.

We can now build a new store in twenty-one days, from the time we sign the lease. On completion of the building of the store, we take seven days to get the drug licence issued after the store has been inspected by the drug inspector. Only after that are we allowed to move products into the store. Stocking and merchandising can take another seven days.

We are therefore up and running within thirty-five days, from the day we sign the lease to the day the first customer walks in. I keep pushing my colleagues to finish this within thirty days since we normally manage to get thirty days 'rent free' from each landlord for fitting out and renovating a store.

Store Formats

Like any other retail chain, we tried several retail formats. Some of the formats we have worked with are:

High street: The largest number of stores we have are located on high streets. These have generally worked well and we have seen a quick ramp-up of sales and consistent growth in our revenue per square foot. These stores have been the mainstay of our operations.

I have also seen significant failures in this format if we did not work within our guidelines of revenue per square foot.

Condominium: Given the huge growth of gated communities and condominium complexes in our country, I decided to enter this space very aggressively. We started with a store in the Laburnum complex in Gurgaon where I live. A residential community offered us direct access to our customers as well as a monopoly inside the community. We now have agreements with most major builders to set up pharmacies inside their residential complexes.

All these stores have worked well. They have broken even, generally within three months of starting operations. The good news about such store formats is that they have limited inventory, since we know the requirements of the community. However, the downside is that these stores achieve their ideal level of sales very quickly and then reach a level of maturity because the customer base is fixed. The level of service required in these stores also has to be of a very high order, given the small community that it serves.

Mall: We tried opening stores in malls, as I had seen in a number of international markets. None of these stores worked as a pharmacy for reasons already discussed.

However, when we launched specialist nutrition and beauty stores inside malls and added a small pharmacy inside such a format, the store worked very well. While the nutrition and beauty products catered to the demands of the customers who visited the mall, the pharmacy was used by the thousands of individuals who worked inside the mall.

BPO: I assumed that any location that had a large number of people would automatically become an excellent location for a Guardian pharmacy. I spoke to a number of my friends who headed large BPOs and arranged to open a store inside their premises. Not even one of these stores worked and we had to close all of them, at a considerable loss to the company.

More recently, I have decided to redo this format and try it again. I refuse to believe that a pharmacy can fail in an environment where the store is a monopoly catering to at least five thousand young men and women.

Store within store: We tried a store-within-a store format with many retailers, starting with a small supermarket chain in Gurgaon under the name Crossroads. The stores did well initially, but we had to close them because the supermarket chain wound up operations because of financial difficulties.

Given this initial success, we signed agreements with

Spencer's, More, Bharti Easy Day and Kendriya Bhandar. We were also approached by a number of other retailers to open a Guardian Pharmacy inside their stores. Barring Kendriya Bhandar, all other formats failed and we had to wind up operations.

When we tried to understand the reason for our failure, we found that the Indian customer was not yet ready to buy medicines when he or she went out shopping for food and grocery products. The other reason for the failure was that our stores were poorly located inside the supermarket with no signage outside. Our Kendriya Bhandar stores worked because all these stores had an independent entrance with a separate signage. Customers were able to identify them with a pharmacy only when they saw them positioned separately with a separate door and a separate set of people managing them.

Fuel stations: Hindustan Petroleum had decided to increase revenue-generating opportunities for their fuel stations and so they invited multiple retail formats to open in them, ranging from food to coffee to books and greeting cards. We decided to experiment with this format, since fuel stations have excellent locations in most cities.

We started with one store in Jaipur, one in Delhi and one in Noida. Hindustan Petroleum realized that ours was the only format that was increasing fuel sales. Customers would come to buy medicines and alongside get their vehicles fuelled, as compared to the other formats where customers would come for fuel and then buy a pizza or a cup of coffee. These stores did well initially and we decided to expand this format quickly.

We selected a number of potential locations from the list provided to us by the company, based on proximity to hospitals and densely populated residential areas. When we asked them to give us documentation for getting the drug licence, we were amazed to find that the company did not have the documentation for a number of its locations. They were unable to find property title deeds in some cases and they did not have agreements which allowed them to open a pharmacy on their premises in others. We were also not able to get proper signage at these fuel stations, even though our agreement provided that we would be given space for them.

We spent a lot of time and money in developing this format but were not able to move forward as we would have liked to. Here was a format that had worked for us, but we had to abandon it because our 'landlord' was not ready.

Later, we were also approached by Bharat Petroleum and Indian Oil, but we politely declined since we knew that the problems we had faced with Hindustan Petroleum would simply be repeated.

Airport: When the new airport terminal in New Delhi, Terminal 1D, was being built, they invited pharmacy chains to open stores inside. Guardian was selected to run the pharmacies at both the departure terminal, 1D, and the arrival terminal, 1C. Our lessons from these stores were unique, since customers at airports had different needs and our stocking pattern had to be changed completely.

Both these stores were very successful and managed to break even in the first month of their operations. It was interesting to see that on the days when Delhi was fogged out resulting in flight delays, our sales would shoot up significantly. Travellers had to wait at the airport and with little else to do, they would shop!

When bids were invited for the latest airport terminal at

New Delhi, Terminal 3, we bid along with other pharmacy chains and once again we were selected to manage three large pharmacies at the International Departures, Domestic Departures and Arrivals.

Because of our success at the Delhi airport, we were invited to open stores at the Hyderabad airport as well. We now have all the three stores at the new Hyderabad airport. Once we had stores at these two airports, we were invited to open a store at the new airport in Mumbai as well. We are also in discussions with a number of other airports in the country.

◆

Several times we have had to close underperforming and loss-incurring stores. Closing a store is never easy, both financially and emotionally. Each time we did so, it felt like a small part of me was dying. However, it is important to close a store rather than let it bleed simply because an entrepreneur is emotionally attached to it.

I have tried to analyse the reasons for the failure of some of our stores and to understand what worked and what did not. In some cases I have managed to get answers for the failure but in most, I am not able to put my finger on the exact reason. Mostly, we ascribe the reasons for failure to poor staff training, poor supplies or simply poor location.

Store Formats—Hospital

A very large segment of the medicines sold in our country are through pharmacies located inside hospitals. All hospitals have at least one in-patient department pharmacy and one out-patient department pharmacy. In addition, they source items that are used in the operation theatres as well as for the hospital's own use. Hospitals also have a separate sourcing arm for more expensive implements—items used in cardiac surgeries and joint replacement surgeries.

In order to grow, I realized that Guardian had to establish a strong presence inside hospitals. When I discussed this strategy with my board members, none of them looked at the hospital pharmacy business very kindly. I explained to them that a pharmacy inside a hospital was simply one more format of our retail stores, and that it made far better business sense to locate a store inside a hospital and cater to the needs of the customers there than be one of many stores outside, but they did not buy the logic.

I went ahead with the store rollout in any case and when my board members started seeing the growth in revenue numbers, they relented and accepted my plan. The topic of retail stores inside hospital pharmacies still comes up for discussion in most of our board meetings!

One brief I give to all my colleagues before we start a retail store inside a hospital is, 'Always remember that for a doctor we will always be a chemist. Never, ever try to upstage a doctor or try and show that we are a large company, because all our business depends on the doctor.'

Sir Sunder Lal Hospital, Banaras Hindu University: Our first hospital store was opened on 4 December 2007 at Sir Sunder Lal Hospital, Banaras Hindu University, in Varanasi. Opening a pharmacy in this hospital was a big challenge and it taught me a lot about dealing with the government. A tender to manage the pharmacy inside the hospital was floated early in the year. Our head of projects took the lead in bidding for this tender. When the tender documents were opened, we had been shortlisted and were called for a series of meetings with the BHU authorities.

Guardian's entry into the fray was not welcomed at all. We were seen as outsiders in the Varanasi market. The local association held protest meetings and even burned my effigy at the local square! The city's chemists called for a one-day strike. But I was determined to fight and get this matter resolved.

Professor Panjab Singh, vice-chancellor of the university, was very decisive and in spite of a lot of negative press and propaganda, he took a decision to award the tender to us, since we were the highest bidders. As happens in a number of government-related tenders where interested parties are involved, one of the unsuccessful bidders filed a stay application in the Allahabad High Court, which was granted. The university authorities worked closely with us and we had the stay vacated from the court before we started our work on renovating the store premises. This store is our biggest yet, with an area of 3,500 square feet and an additional 5,000 square feet of customer waiting areas. The store has sixteen checkout counters and handles over 1,500 customers a day.

I learnt a new terminology called 'Propaganda Medicines' when we started operations in hospitals in Uttar Pradesh. This term is used to refer to instances where the doctor prescribes the medicines of a specific company and these are available only at a specific chemist, thereby controlling the margins from the manufacturer to the retailer. The practice of propaganda medicines is prevalent all over the country. Guardian has not been able to make a breakthrough with such manufacturers to stock these medicines, since the vested interests don't want organized retail to enter this area.

Like my first store in Galleria, BHU was my first retail pharmacy inside a hospital and I have a strong emotional connect with this store and its management team. It has also helped

Guardian build a strong competency in managing hospital pharmacies and using this base, we have managed to acquire many more spaces in hospitals in India.

Government hospital: Buoyed by our experience in Varanasi, we participated in a tender in November 2008 to manage the pharmacies of all six medical colleges of the Government of Uttar Pradesh and we were fortunate enough to win this.

We now operate pharmacies inside all the medical colleges in Gorakhpur, Jhansi, Meerut, Agra, Kanpur and Allahabad. We have learned how to handle the requirements of various government authorities and have received hundreds of letters and comments from satisfied customers from rural India, commending us for the reliability of the medicines that we sell as well as the price protection guarantee that we offer.

We have also been contacted by several other states to discuss the possibility of managing the pharmacies in their state-owned medical colleges.

Trust and charitable hospital: I approached Yogi Durlabhji, managing trustee of the Santokhba Durlabhji Memorial Hospital (SDMH) in Jaipur, to give us an opportunity to manage his hospital pharmacies.

SDMH is the second-largest hospital in Jaipur after the government-owned Sawai Madho Singh Hospital. It has over five hundred beds and caters to the large community of Jaipur and the neighbouring districts. During the Jaipur bomb blasts in 2008, my colleagues opened up the pharmacies inside the hospital and gave away free medicines. We ensured that we stood by the hospital as it went about healing hundreds of victims.

Our early mistakes in Jaipur taught us a lot about working with hospital managements.

Private hospital: Even though we had managed to get a foothold into government-owned hospitals and charitable hospitals, we were not being able to make a breakthrough into the very large and growing private hospitals.

I started meeting everyone I knew who owned a hospital or was even remotely connected with a private hospital, no matter how large or small. My colleagues and I must have made dozens of presentations to hospital owners in various cities, but getting a breakthrough was a huge challenge.

Medanta, the Medicity, in Gurgaon, is the dream project of Dr Naresh Trehan. It aims to eventually have 1,600 beds and will become the largest private hospital in Asia. Chatting with Dr Trehan was an education in itself. I was fascinated with his vision for health. I remember his words: 'Outsourcing means that you have to ensure I get what I would normally have earned and you meet your costs through improved efficiencies and your scale of operations. I will give you a chance to manage my pharmacy, provided you don't attempt to profit from this. Work with me for the long run and you will do well.'

In 2010, we negotiated on having stores inside his hospital. I was ready to accept all his terms because I knew that he is the 'gold standard' in health. Once he took a decision, we signed the agreement within twenty-four hours.

A number of hospital owners from around the country have now started talking to us to manage their pharmacies. Their logic seems to be simple—if Dr Trehan has found it worth his while to outsource to Guardian, then he must have done this with a lot of thought and foresight.

Deals with many more hospitals, including Vinayak Hospital in Noida, Sarvodaya Hospital in Faridabad, Pushpanjali Hospital in Agra, Merrygold Hospital in Agra, Rajputana Hospital in

Jaipur and Bhagwati Hospital in New Delhi and others were signed in quick succession from 2009 onwards.

Managing all these hospital owners and promoters is a task that I handle personally. Over a period of time, though, I know that this relationship will be managed through the respective management teams of both organizations.

Guardian now manages the pharmacies in twenty-six hospitals, which have more than 11,500 beds put together, making us the largest hospital pharmacy player in the country.

Store Formats—Rural

I wanted to go into rural India because I genuinely thought that we would be able to make a big difference by selling reliable medicines to the people living there.

Ajay Shriram, who was setting up Hariyali Kissan Bazaar stores in rural and semi-urban India, agreed to open an Aushadhi store on a pilot basis in one of his outlets located in Kairthal, Rajasthan.

I personally worked on the designing and stocking of this store. In order to make our customers identify with our store, I asked a well-known photographer to take a series of photographs from some villages in India to be displayed inside. We launched the pharmacy with a lot of fanfare and the press gave us a lot of coverage because we were addressing the 'bottom of the pyramid'.

However, our experiment did not work and after sustaining losses for almost one year, we decided to close the store.

The lessons we learnt from this experiment were:

- The market at the bottom of the pyramid is very fragmented, given the large number of villages that need to be covered. We should have recognized that if an urban customer wants a pharmacy close to where he lives, the needs of a rural consumer would not be any different.

- Getting qualified store staff to work in rural India proved to be a huge challenge. We even tried to hire people from the same village, but the moment they would get a job with us, their personal aspirations would rise and they would want a career in the city. We were not able to get long-term employees at the store.

- Supplies to the store became a huge challenge and a very expensive exercise. We had to deliver from either Gurgaon or Jaipur to ensure the quality of medicines, and the cost of delivery became higher than the margins we would make, given the low sales of the store.

- The local chemist who had been operating in the village for several years, possibly for more than one generation, had a personal bond of trust with all his customers. He would give medicines on credit and had his own unique system of recovering the money. While we were able to handle the issue of trust from our customers, we were not able to handle the issue of 'payable when able' basis.

- Managing a store in a remote location became a big challenge for all the service functions from the company's headquarters. Audit of the stocks inside the store was the first to be affected. Deposit of cash sales was the second problem as we were not able to monitor cash deposits regularly.

- Finally, getting one of our operations lead to visit the store to oversee the functioning became a serious problem as well, which resulted in the store operating pretty much on its own for several weeks at a time.

MARKETING

But, the thing is, since I always had my own little shop and direct access to the public, I've been able to build up a technique without marketing people ever telling me what the public wants.

—Vivienne Westwood, fashion designer

Marketing a health service brand is always a challenge, since it takes many years to build the value proposition of the brand in the minds of customers. I recognized this from the beginning and took a decision to invest in the Guardian brand in more ways than one. I had chosen '100% Reliable' as our positioning platform and knew that getting this message across would be tough in the short term.

Today, as I look back, I realize that though the journey has been difficult, we have established Guardian as a provider of 100 per cent reliable medicines. While every chain and every store selling medicines makes the same claim, our investment in this platform for the last ten years has begun to pay dividends. I was pleasantly surprised to hear from a number of customers that their doctors would tell them, 'If you have purchased your medicine at a Guardian store, you don't need to come back and show it to us. We trust Guardian.'

We could not have asked for a stronger endorsement.

A retail pharmacy chain works with the customers that

live in its immediate surroundings and Guardian spends all its marketing money in the neighbourhoods where our stores are located, working with the communities we serve.

In order to reach out to the large residential communities that our stores seek to serve, I had to think out of the box. Getting attention in the clutter is difficult and spending large sums of money on local, regional or national media is unwise in the early days of a retail pharmacy.

In order to write good advertisements to communicate with customers, it is important to work with an advertising agency that understands the requirements. Like most growing companies, my needs and more importantly, my understanding of our own business was changing every day.

Leaflets and Banners

The most common way, used by small businesses in local neighbourhoods, to reach out to customers is to use leaflets that are inserted into their morning newspaper by the newspaper vendor. It costs money to print the leaflet as well as to have it inserted. There is a lot of uncertainty whether the leaflet will be inserted at all, even if you have paid for it, since the newspaper vendors do this early in the morning under severe time pressure. Most newspaper readers I know, including Vera, instruct their domestic help to 'shake' the newspaper outside the door to rid it of all these 'irritating leaflets that don't let you read the newspaper peacefully' before it is delivered to them. Thus the brand, via this medium of newspaper inserts, is not even able to reach the customer, let alone have its communication read.

I used this format to announce some of our promotions in the early years, in 2004 and 2005, and in order to ensure that the leaflets were inserted properly, I visited the collection and distribution point of the newspapers at 4 a.m. Even then I could not ensure that they were inserted properly because of the speed at which it was done. The newspaper vendors were in a hurry to deliver the newspaper to the readers on time and insertion of leaflets, while an additional source of income, was an irritant and slowed down their primary task of delivering the newspapers.

The other popular form of getting consumers' attention is to use banners. These banners clutter up a neighbourhood, though, and light poles, which are used to string them, can be seen covered with threads of varying colours. We too tried this medium but stopped when we found that we were violating local municipal regulations.

Guardian Health Chronicle

Rajiv Verma, chief executive officer (CEO) of the *Hindustan Times,* suggested that we should consider doing our own newspaper, which would be inserted by their company in their newspaper at their printing press and thus save us from the uncertainty associated with the leaflet insertion by the newspaper vendor.

The idea of setting up my own newspaper with the Guardian brand name on the masthead was very exciting indeed.

I decided to name the newspaper *Guardian Health Chronicle.* We agreed to publish the newspaper every alternative Thursday as a health supplement with the *Hindustan Times.* It was planned as a four-page broadsheet printed on regular newsprint to give it a look and feel similar to the daily newspaper. The first newspaper was published on 4 January 2006.

In order to reach out to our Hindi-speaking customers, I decided that we must launch a Hindi edition of the *Guardian*

Health Chronicle and entered into an agreement with *Dainik Jagran*. The Hindi edition was launched on 15 June 2006.

Both the English and the Hindi editions were very successful in building the Guardian brand as a srong health service brand across North India.

Where we failed in this venture was in our inability to raise advertising revenues to pay for the cost of this newspaper, and while we continue to support the initiative as a marketing exercise, I know that some advertising revenue would help us invest further in the product and increase circulation.

After publishing the newspaper for six years we decided to change the format to a magazine. This was done because based on consumer feedback we realized that though a newspaper has a strong value add for the brand, it has a limited shelf life of one day. A magazine, on the other hand, would have a shelf life of one month. Our magazine became successful only because we had invested six years in building the brand via the newspaper.

We have also been asked to consider bringing out a booklet every year, which would include the best articles from the *Guardian Health Chronicle*.

Guardian XtraValu Advantage Card

Like most retail chains, we too decided that Guardian must have its own loyalty programme. This programme would give loyalty points to our customers on all their purchases at Guardian stores. It has gone through several changes as we learned more about our customers' expectations as well as our own ability to manage this programme. We run several promotions for our cardholders, including extra loyalty points during certain weeks of each month, special discounts on Guardian-branded products, and so on.

We now have over 350,000 members of the Guardian XtraValu Advantage card and are adding over ten thousand members each month. The card has been a huge success with our customers and we find that a very high number of them shop repeatedly at our stores.

The database for this programme is always kept on highly secure servers with restricted access, both because we wish to protect the privacy of our customers as well as because of the value that a database provides in its ability to access targeted customers. We are now able to 'slice and dice' this database in many ways to understand what our customers expect from Guardian.

We have upgraded the offerings under this loyalty programme consistently and, based on a recent IMRB survey, I was delighted to learn that our XtraValu card offers the best programme to customers and our customers feel that Guardian offered them the best deals in the market.

Radio and Television Advertising

As the chain started to expand, we decided to experiment with radio and television advertising to understand its impact. We tried a few spots on local channels and this did create a little buzz about the company.

However, I found out that mass media does not work for a small retail chain because of the highly localized nature of our offering, but I had to spend money to understand this better. Radio and television spots did not bring any additional footfalls into our stores, even when we offered attractive prizes, like trips for two to Bangkok or a 42-inch television.

We also tried advertising on cable channels in residential colonies. After not getting any response, we tried to understand why this had failed. We found that in most homes, cable channels were no longer being watched by the decision-makers, but by domestic help. We were reaching out to viewers who had no decision-making authority to buy at Guardian stores. We then stopped all mass media advertising and reverted to our below-the-line marketing plans for reaching out to our customers directly.

As the chain is growing in reach, we are now once again planning to test the radio in the National Capital Region as a means to reach out to customers, this time primarily for messages such as 'free home delivery' and special schemes for our senior citizens.

Camps

We regularly conduct camps in association with resident welfare associations, schools and office complexes, because this is the simplest and most direct way to reach out to customers near their homes.

We have held camps in parks at 5 a.m. for morning walkers and joggers to check health symptoms related to blood sugar and blood pressure, we have held camps with nutritionists in residential complexes to design diet charts for residents and we have held beauty camps at clubs for ladies coming to attend kitty parties.

Guardian camps have also helped us build our credibility with our customers. The only problem with holding such camps is that these are very people-intensive and costly.

Home Delivery

As customers get busier at their workplaces and families move towards dual incomes with lesser support at home, we find that demands for home delivery of products is growing rapidly, and all our stores offer this facility. This facility is also offered by food retail and a number of other retail formats.

I was faced with an interesting dilemma when we first launched home delivery service. We received a call from the local drug inspector asking us to stop this service, since home delivery of medicines was not permitted under the law. When I asked him why the response I got was interesting: 'Under the drug licence granted to you, only a licensed individual can sell medicines after seeing a valid prescription and you are sending medicines with a delivery boy.'

To this I responded, 'I can ask my pharmacist to deliver the medicines. The pharmacist, who is qualified, can see the prescription and then hand them over.'

He obviously knew the law much better than I did because he countered, 'Yes but your drug licence is only to sell medicines in your licensed premises; and further, under the Indian Contract Act of 1872, a sale takes place when money is exchanged and you are taking cash when you hand over the medicines.'

Over the last few years the drug department has become far more receptive to the needs of patients and Guardian does provide home delivery services, but only after ensuring that all the legal aspects have been complied with.

E-Marketing

A few years back, seeing the growing presence of people online, we decided to use the Internet to approach our customers. We did this in stages, given the resources we had, and to coincide with the network of stores, which was slowly beginning to grow. My objective in developing this was to ensure that our brand remained contemporary.

Website development: The first thing any entrepreneur needs to do is to get his company's website up and running. We first registered *www.guardianlifecare.com* and thereafter, as the number of business offerings started to get larger, we added *www.guardianntrition.in* and *www.myhealthguardian.com*. We are now launching home delivery through a separate website, *www. guardianrx.in*. To integrate all of them into a larger corporate website, we created *www.guardian.in*.

After we launched *Guardian Health Chronicle*, we decided that in order to reach a larger audience, we should build an electronic edition. We got this website completed in record time. Our customers can now access information on health, classified by different health needs of our customer base. We also keep inviting our customers to send us articles, as well as give us inputs on a regular basis to expand the website content.

More recently, we have started a weekly emailer to all our registered customers, in which we cover multiple subjects under the titles of Guardian Wellness, Guardian Nutrition and Guardian Beauty. Each subject is covered once a week by rotation.

Ecommerce: In order to create a virtual store, we added a facility for our customers to place orders on our website. But the laws of our country did not permit sale of medicines in any location other than a licensed store. We therefore started by selling only our nutrition and beauty products, and our non-pharmaceutical Guardian brands, online. Over the past few years the laws of the land have started to recognize the customers' need and Guardian has started selling medicines based through its website, but only after receiving a prescription from the customer first.

Blog: The Guardian blog was created much after the website. It is now running at *www.myheathguardian.blogspot.com*.

Facebook/Twitter: Recognizing the huge potential of the social media space, we started to tweet under the handle @askguardian and quickly had a long list of loyal followers who engage with us on a regular basis. I also tweet under my own handle @gargashutosh. Further, Guardian started to become active on Facebook as well. We keep running competitions to engage with our customers on an ongoing basis.

Bundled Offers

In order to give value-based offers to our customers, we have bundled different products together so that customers get a range of complementary products at the best possible prices. We have always received excellent feedback from our customers for such bundled offers.

Buy One Get One (BOGO): We experimented with a Buy One Get One offer on our entire range of Guardian Ayurveda juices. This offer was taken up very quickly by our customers. When we tried to withdraw it, we found that the sale of juices dropped. Though we knew that the customers were getting good value for money on these juices even without the offer, the fact that our sales dropped meant that we had to listen to our customers more. We reinstated the scheme and have made this offer permanent, as demanded by our customers.

Linked offers and complementary products: We also launched linked offers—products that complement each other from different companies. To this end we linked products from nutrition and wellness firms such as GNC with multiple products from large FMCG companies. For example, we would sell a GNC hair, skin and nails' vitamin with another brand's shampoo, or a GNC Fish Oil antioxidant with a skin cream, to convey to the customer the advantages of using vitamins for general wellness.

In addition, we offered several complementary products such as Guardian Glucose with Guardian XtrAqua Mineral Water or Xtra Muscle Whey Protein along with Xtra Muscle Glucosamine. We did this since the usage of such products complement one another.

We also launched a set of four of our Ayurveda juices in a combo pack for Diwali at attractive prices with the tag line 'Gift Health this Diwali'. This was well received by our customers and we sold hundreds of these during the festive season.

HUMAN RESOURCES

My main job was developing talent. I was a gardener providing water and other nourishment to our top 750 people. Of course, I had to pull out some weeds, too.

—Jack Welch, former chairman and CEO, General Electric

The human resource (HR) function of any retail company can make it or break it, since retail companies are people-intensive and our people are our ambassadors and the 'face' for our customers. This function must have a strong leader and needs complete support from the entrepreneur.

Setting the Management Culture

The entrepreneur must outline his philosophy for the managerial function in words and in deeds, because this is what will set the management culture of the company. Since I am the oldest member of the Guardian management, I often had to stop younger managers from touching my feet and 'seeking my blessings'. I would tell them that there is no need to do so, no matter what the culture of our country may be. If I had allowed this to continue, other senior managers would have expected similar behaviour from their juniors.

Each time I walked into a manager's room or I walked down an office aisle, people would stop their work and stand up. I have never understood how stopping work and standing is a way of showing respect to a senior. To me, continuing with your work when a manager walks down the aisle is a much stronger way of respecting the senior individual as well as the organization. It has taken me time, but the message in Guardian is very clear—continue with your work when a senior manager happens to walk past you and keep sitting in your chair if a senior walks into your office.

The foundation day of the company—25 August—is celebrated as the Guardian anniversary where we honour our top performers of the previous year.

Some of the guiding HR principles that I established very early in our development were:

- Guardian would rapidly move towards professional management and we would not build a family-run organization.
- We would aim for professional growth based on meritocracy and not on relationships or patronage.
- Any relationships between managers would need to be disclosed at the time of hiring and approved by the management committee of the company. We also specified that two managers who were related to each other would not be allowed to work in the same department.
- Performance would be evaluated based on agreed and quantifiable key result areas (KRAs) for each manager.
- Salary increments would be based on achievement of results, not seniority.
- While I was clear that the company would never interfere in the personal lives of employees, if it is found that a male and female employee were dating, one of them would be asked to leave.

Implement HR Policies That You Are Willing to Live with Yourself

In large established companies, HR policies are followed because 'everyone else' follows them and no one asks for any exceptions to be made. However, in a new company, most new employees try and implement policies they have either seen in use elsewhere or want to get implemented for their own needs.

I made it clear to everyone that we would only implement those policies for our employees that I was willing to accept myself. I took a decision to abide with the policies of the HR department in their entirety so that there would no exceptions:

- I mark my attendance on the biometric fingerprint reader every morning and evening.
- I ask for leave in the standard company-approved application form.
- I ensure that I pay for all my purchases from a Guardian store and that no discounts are given to me.
- If I call for any samples, these have to be duly authorized.
- All my expense claims are approved by another board member.
- I fly economy class and stay at hotels that are listed in the company manual for my level.

Only when people started to see me following the company's policies did they also accept these and adhered to them.

Good People Are Needed by a Startup but They Won't Join

One of the biggest dilemmas I was faced with as I built Guardian was that the company needed good management people, but the most competent people were not willing to join a startup.

I found it a huge challenge to get strong professional

managers to leave large companies and join us. Good managers, I realized, are generally poor risk-takers. Only when they see the stability of a company or other professional managers taking this leap of faith do they agree to make a change. This meant that we had to keep hiring good people to take the company to a certain level, and at regular points of our growth, we had to keep upgrading our skill sets as the company needed more skilled people.

I would often be asked by potential investors why we were changing so many middle-management people and though I tried, I don't think I was able to explain to them well enough that for every startup, barring a few outstanding managers, it is healthy to keep changing people and upgrading the skill sets.

These rapid changes were happening not because I wanted to change managers or because they did not want to work for Guardian, but simply because good people were not willing to work for a startup that neither offered much career guarantee nor significantly higher compensation packages.

Pay as Per the Market, Not Higher

Sir James Goldsmith, an Anglo-French businessman, publisher and politician said, 'You pay peanuts and you get monkeys.'

While this may be a politically incorrect statement, it epitomizes the thought that every entrepreneur is faced with when he has to take a decision on how to fix salary levels of the employees in the early days.

While I could gauge the salary level of our store staff, based on a quick round of other shops and asking people, I was always faced with a challenge while determining the salary levels of middle management and senior management. I was never certain about what the person's current salary levels were because everyone I interviewed was 'expecting' a promotion in the next two months and a salary hike of at least 40 per cent.

I set up a system of speaking to other leaders in the retail industry for a reference check on the individual and to understand what they were offering potential employees. More importantly, I decided test how far the employee was willing to compromise in his negotiation. More often than not, we would arrive at an understanding halfway between the employee's expectations and our offer. Only in a few cases did a potential hire not come back to us because the compensation was not enough.

Manage Manpower Numbers Carefully

Manpower numbers, if not controlled, can very easily spiral in a new company.

During Guardian's early days, my colleagues sometimes caught me in the office corridor and asked me to sanction an additional person. Without thinking, I may have nodded or given my acceptance to several such appointments. Before I knew it, every department had hired more people than they needed. They wanted to build redundancy at every level so that they would not have a problem if one person resigned. Their reason was logical; however, this redundancy was expensive and extra people resulted in poor efficiency for the entire department. No one seemed to know who was responsible for what and everyone waited for someone else to take action, because there was always someone else to blame.

We had to quickly implement manpower plans for each department and ensure that the function heads justified every individual that they wanted in their departments. The HR head was given a budget both for manpower numbers and manpower cost.

Similarly, every area manager and every store manager wanted extra people in their stores and their justification, to be able to offer 'better customer service'. In order to understand their requirements and to be fair to each store, we developed productivity norms wherein we established revenue per employee across different locations and different classes of stores. Stores that were performing better were given extra manpower. This way, we were able to reduce almost 10 per cent of our staff strength.

Professionalize, But in Time

While it must always be the objective of every entrepreneur who is working towards building a big business on a national level to bring in strong professionals and gradually hand over the operations to them, the timing of bringing them in has to be right. As a manager turned entrepreneur myself, I was acutely aware that I must bring in a professional manager.

A few years after starting, I decided that in the interest of the company, I would start stepping back by bringing in a president. When the person I appointed to head the company joined, the first thing he did was to spend a lot of money in renovating his office. While I had simple metal doors with glass windows, he got his office walls lined with wood panelling, fixed expensive blinds on his windows, changed his air conditioner and ordered the latest laptop.

He made a commitment to the board at a presentation that Guardian would achieve certain operating parameters. Instead of focusing on these and building the business, his focus shifted to building small groups of loyal people in different cities. He would schedule a meeting with area managers and call them at a certain time. If they were late by more than thirty minutes, he would refuse to see them and send them away without even enquiring about the reason for delay.

On one occasion, he called our area manager from Jaipur for a meeting at 10 a.m. This person must have taken the overnight bus from Jaipur to Gurgaon, and he reached our office at 11.30 a.m. He was told to go back to Jaipur without meeting the boss because he was late.

The president generally worked around his diary and scheduled every appointment a few weeks in advance. While this was a very good practice and would have served him well in a well-established corporate setup, it was impossible to be a stickler for timing in a startup company, that too in retail, where there are fires to be put out every day.

Another time, I asked him if he could come over to my room, adjacent to his, for an unscheduled meeting, since something urgent had come up. He looked at me and said nothing. Then he went to his room, called me over the intercom and said, 'I think I can slot you in for a meeting for fifteen minutes post lunch.'

The performance of the company declined since he had time for everything except running stores. People started resigning because he had no time to listen to them and was not addressing their problems.

I had to ask him to leave and took executive control of the company once again.

So much for professional managers!

While it is important to professionalize a startup, handing over the reins should only be done when the organization has built sufficient resilience to handle the changes that a professional manager is bound to bring in for the long-term good of the company. I probably appointed a president earlier than I should have.

Retain Key Talent 'At All Costs'

Early on, I started to identify key managers whom I categorized as 'retain at all costs'. These were not linked to any role or position. My benchmark for identifying them was to look for individuals who would go beyond the call of duty for Guardian.

I have told my colleagues in HR that we must anticipate the needs of such individuals. Their compensation and career progression is planned in advance, because these people are really the future leaders.

As the organization grows, we keep adding more names to this category and over the next few years, I am confident that a strong Guardian culture will start to evolve.

Delegate and Trust

I have always believed in empowering my colleagues, both as a professional manager as well as an entrepreneur. I keep telling my senior colleagues that the earlier they are able to run the company without me around, the sooner I will delegate more authority so that I will have more time to focus on strategic thinking. However, delegation of authority must be done carefully and slowly, since a startup faces much vulnerability and strong hands are needed to steer it through its early years. Two lessons that I have learnt in this respect are:

Empower with accountability: A lot of managers want the authority to take decisions, but do not want the accountability that goes with this.

Trust slowly and carefully: I have consistently been given one feedback in all my appraisals as a professional manager: that I tend to trust people more than I should. While I think this is a positive trait, I have been let down several times by colleagues. This has led me to believe that while trust is the foundation of every working relationship, it must be reposed slowly and sparingly.

Training Is Critical

I have always given importance to training our store staff and our operations leadership. Without a well-trained team, Guardian will struggle to show that our stores are different from the neighbourhood chemist shop.

We have set up a 'training store' in our corporate office where new entrants are trained in actual work-like situations and pharmacists are asked to fill in actual prescriptions. We have requested some doctors to write prescriptions for us in different types of handwriting since a lot of doctors write fairly illegibly and it is the job of the pharmacist to decipher this quickly.

Our training ranges from basic personal hygiene tips to handling the point-of-sale computer system; from simple customer-care tips to upselling and cross-selling.

When I speak to our young retail staff at the end of each training session, I always conclude with the words, 'When you work in a retail store, every morning when you leave for work, take off your ego and hang it on the hook behind your bathroom door at home. Then take off your watch and leave it on your bedside table.'

There is no place for either your ego or your watch in a store. You cannot argue with a customer simply because he shouts at you. At the same time, you cannot ask a customer to leave your store because he is browsing when your shift has ended.

Discipline

It is critical to maintain discipline at stores, be it timings or wearing uniforms while on duty. Indiscipline can have the far-reaching ramifications across the organization.

Two instances will help demonstrate how we handled the matter of discipline at stores:

Once, we discovered that a large amount of cash had been stolen by one of the senior staff members in one of the stores. I asked our chief financial officer (CFO) and operations head to rush to the location and filed a police report immediately. We managed to gain access to the concerned staff member's bank accounts where he had been depositing large sums of cash every day. On confronting him, we were threatened with the standard line most Indians use when in trouble, 'Don't you know who I am and don't you know who I know?' Using the large deposits in his bank account as evidence, we got him arrested by the local police. When political pressure to get him released did not work, within a few hours the family members of the concerned employee came to us and returned all the money with a request that we withdraw the police complaint.

In another incident, when a shortfall of cash was noticed in a store by the company's internal audit team, the three staff members at the store decided to take the law in their own hands. When six of the senior managers from the head office went to the store, the store staff called thirty goons from the city, locked up their senior colleagues and beat them up. They also demanded money from the company to release the managers. The only way for me to tackle this head-on was to get into my car, drive to the city and meet the police and lawyers. My going to the store with the police and our lawyers was seen as a very positive sign by the employees across the organization. One of the three employees turned approver while we filed a criminal case against the other two. The money that was stolen, however, was never recovered.

Employee Stock Options

It was my belief that if employees in the company were able to buy company shares they would have a much greater sense of ownership. Owning shares of the company that they worked in would also enable the employees to create wealth for themselves. Even before we started operations of the company, I took a decision that we would set aside 5 per cent of the company shares for our employee stock option plan (ESOP). Shares would be given to employees based on their seniority, their performance and their commitment to Guardian.

We applied to the Central Board of Direct Taxes and got our ESOP scheme approved.

However, Guardian was an unlisted company and unlike listed companies where employees could easily sell their shares on the stock market, I realized that our employees would not be able to sell their Guardian shares. In order to make the ESOP scheme of an unlisted company attractive to our employees, I announced that the company would be the market maker and would fix a price to purchase the shares at the end of each financial year in case an employee wanted to cash in on his options once we were entitled. We established that the employee would be able to surrender his vested shares and take the differential profit accrued to him from the company.

I learned the following once we had announced our ESOP scheme:

- Junior employees did not understand the meaning or value of their company's shares. All they wanted was an increase in their salary. They did not understand the potential of owning a stake in the company. I further realized that the attrition in the junior employees was very high and therefore waiting for a long period to accrue and then encash their shares was not attractive for them.
- Middle-level management employees wanted to own shares, but were unsure of how long they would stay with the company or how long it would take the company to get listed, so that they could realize the value of these shares.
- Senior managers were the only group who understood the value of being able to own company shares. In addition to their commitment to the organization, they were also aware of its valuation based on the successive rounds of funding, so they could see the value of their 'right' rapidly multiplying.

A few years later I invited Tarun Gulati, founder of an organization called 'just ESOPs', to redevelop a comprehensive ESOP scheme for the company. I told him that the scheme should be attractive enough to offer a wealth creation of between four to six times the current cost to company (CTC) for each eligible employee in the next four years. This time we decided that only senior management would be entitled to the ESOP scheme.

Personal Hygiene and Dress Code

Ensuring personal hygiene was another challenge we faced in our early days. I would see some of our store staff with a bright orange mark on their foreheads on Tuesday since they had visited Lord Hanuman's temple, or sporting a stubble on Thursday, or other similar religious marks. I have nothing against any religion and respect all faiths. The employees are free to exercise their free will in this matter, but I was clear that religious symbolisms would not be permitted inside the company's store. If any employee insisted on carrying out rituals, they could take leave on that particular day. We had a small uproar initially but when I stuck to my decision, all these practices stopped.

The only exception that we have made is for our Islamic staff members, who are permitted to grow their beards if they wish to during the holy month of Ramadan. Other employees can also sport well-maintained beards, but are not permitted unshaven faces.

Dress code: We do not allow staff to wear any casual clothes to work. In addition, we do not allow our male staff to wear sandals or slippers. All staff members are required to wear company-issued lab coats when on duty in a store. At our head office, we have permitted staff members to wear casual clothes to work only on Fridays.

Sometimes, I found some staff members wearing unwashed clothes, resulting in strong body odour. It took time for them to understand that they had to wear clean clothes not because I wanted them to but for personal hygiene, as well out of respect to our customers.

KRA Setting and Appraisals

When it was time for the annual appraisals, I found that a lot of senior managers did not like to confront their subordinates, especially when they had to give negative feedback. I was often faced with a scenario of getting negative feedback about a manager throughout the year and then finding that the same person had been recommended for a larger than normal increment or a promotion. When I would ask the senior management the reason for this dissonance, they would say, 'Boss, it is finally your call. We will go by whatever you tell us to do.'

It took me a while to convince them that I could not conduct appraisals or take arbitrary decisions for managers reporting to them, and that tough calls had to be taken by each one of them, not me alone.

Over the last two years, we have ensured that the KRAs are attached to the increment letter for every employee, so that they are clear on what is expected of them in the coming year.

Profit Sharing at Store

In order to get our store staff to commit to bottom lines and to give them a share in the success of their stores, we decided to test out a profit-sharing approach. We would share an agreed percentage of monthly profits with them if they could:

- Increase sales.
- Increase revenue per customer.
- Push the sales of Guardian brands to improve margins.
- Reduce pilferage of stocks.
- Reduce wasteful expenditure.
- Manage inventory better.
- Manage company assets with more care.

This profit-sharing scheme worked in a few stores but did not work in some. Well-trained store staff took up the challenge of improving store performance and hence increased their earnings, while the poorly trained ones adopted an 'I could not care less' attitude.

We withdrew the scheme and decided to re-launch it when we were better prepared.

Damini—Redressal Mechanism for Women Employees

Recognizing the large proportion of female employees, I asked our HR head to set up a redressal mechanism for them. We constituted a four-person team led by one of the senior lady managers and including other lady employees. This forum was christened 'Damini'.

'Maine Socha' (I Thought) Syndrome

These two words are possibly the most misused ones in the Hindi lexicon. They are used to cover up mistakes that people make without taking the responsibility that goes with taking a decision.

I often tell my colleagues that we must avoid using the words 'maine socha' (I thought) too often when a decision they have taken has gone wrong. How often have we asked an individual to go from point A to point B to point C and then point D and found that the instructions have not been carried out because the person started from point A, went to point D and then came back, messing up the entire sequence.

When questioned, the standard answer is, 'Maine socha (I thought) I would do this differently.'

Senior Management

Successful businesses can only be built by strong and secure management teams. Such teams are hard to find. Just because an individual has started a company does not mean that he has all the answers. The promoter of any business is also human and will make mistakes.

One of the practices I have followed with my senior colleagues from the very beginning was to over-communicate with them. I share virtually everything relating to the operations of the company with them. I have found that the more I share, the more responsibility they take because they know that there is nothing hidden from them and more often than not, they come up with innovative ways to resolve ticklish issues.

Strong management teams must have the conviction to disagree with the promoter, and good promoters must be secure enough to accept this. I am blessed to have a few good colleagues who treat Guardian as their own baby.

I have often told my senior colleagues that the promoter of the company does not have the luxury of resigning and walking away if the going gets tough. We just have to dig our heels in and make the best of the situation.

Board of Directors

Every leader starts out by leading himself first. I have often seen entrepreneurs pack their boards with family members whom they can control. This removes the normal checks and balances that every organization needs; neither does it foster an environment of strong governance practices. A board of directors must be able to separate ownership from governance. If board members keep discussing the valuation of their shares, when would they work on governance and direction, which are needed to increase the valuation?

An independent board of directors that shares your vision is a dream for every entrepreneur.

At Guardian, while formal board meetings are held four times a year as per the law, we also have at least two annual board conference calls. In addition, I know that I can always speak to any of my board members on the phone at any time. We have disagreements and arguments, but at the end of each meeting we come out with a stronger organization, more focus and with greater clarity on where we are headed.

Vera is on the board of directors of all our companies and supports my decisions. I have come to respect her sixth sense about people after so many years of being together.

Management Team

I started off like most startups do—with qualified people working on a part-time basis. In addition, I had to hire a lot of employees who did not necessarily have the skill sets I was looking for, but I had to compromise because of payment constraints. This put much more pressure on me since I would end up doing mundane tasks such as correcting letters and going through every word of an advertisement.

Putting together a top management team for any startup is always a huge challenge. It is important to get good professionals who are ambitions and hungry for growth.

A major challenge that I have consistently faced with some members of top management is their complete lack of desire to tackle problems. These people want to function as 'auditors' and whenever they visit a store or a warehouse, they come back to me with a list of all the problems that they have seen, instead of tackling the issues head-on. When I ask them to come up with answers to resolve the problem they look at me blankly. The moment the going gets a little tough, such managers either want a change of role or they simply resign.

Putting the monkey on my back is very easy. Most senior managers work on a document and then send it to me with a request that I should have a 'quick look at it' or simply 'glance at it'. The moment this document is sent to me, the manager has absolved himself or herself from responsibility. I now have to read through the complete document carefully to give my comments because if something goes wrong, the manager will quite easily state, 'But I sent the document to you and you approved it!'

When I asked some professional managers to join Guardian in our early days, the standard responses were either that Guardian could not afford their salaries or the company did not offer them enough challenge. Times have changed now and we get a lot of people enquiring about job opportunities with us.

I did manage to put together a good team and several of my colleagues, who have been with Guardian since its inception, are indispensable to the company.

Without them, Guardian would never have been built.

Top Management

A strong, no-nonsense CEO makes all the difference, especially for a retail company, where there are fires to put out every day in multiple locations.

At the same time, getting a strong CFO is a huge challenge for every startup. The company needs strong financial systems, but in their early days most companies do not have the ability to pay for good talent.

The relationship between a CEO and a CFO has to be one of trust and mutual respect. The CFO must be strong enough to advise and guide the CEO in taking decisions and make his views known wherever he disagrees. A CEO must encourage such dissension. However, once a decision has been arrived at, the two of them must be able to close ranks and move forward as a team. Without this bond between the two, building a strong company will always prove to be a challenge.

However, the ultimate responsibility of the company lies with me, both as the chairman and the promoter, and I have to ensure that all checks and balances are in place to monitor and run our operations.

Legal Matters

Give me the bad news first.

This is the request I always make to all my colleagues. Covering up bad news is not going to work in the long run because if the issue is not resolved, it will blow up and when matters come to a head, the problem will reach my desk and I will have to intervene at a late stage. If I get to know about the problem in advance, I can take steps to resolve the matter or take corrective action in time.

I have generally tried to keep Guardian away from litigation because lawsuits are very expensive and time-consuming, and direct a company's energy into unproductive areas. Yet, I am not suggesting that if you are being wronged, you should shy away from a court battle. If one does get involved in legal matters, it is critical to work with legal counsel you can trust and who understand the nature and requirements of your business. Unless there is trust, mutual understanding and respect, there will always be differing opinions on legal matters, which may result in incorrect decisions being taken in the long run.

It is generally advisable to have in-house counsel for most small and medium-sized companies. Quick advice becomes a necessity once a company's business starts to expand. While external opinion is generally advisable, an internal viewpoint needs to be developed before external counsel is consulted.

Family Members—a Huge Asset for a Startup

I have consistently maintained that Guardian must be built as a strong professional company based on a platform of meritocracy, and that only people who perform should be offered bigger roles. I also believe that only a strong management culture with motivated teams who can foresee growth in the company will drive any new business towards institutionalizing itself.

However, I have started to realize the merits of having family members as part of the business, and why most successful family business promoters bring in their family members into the business as early as possible.

I do not have the luxury of family members working alongside me at the moment since both my sons are working for large multinationals. None of my other family members seem to be interested in joining Guardian either

However, I do hope that someday one or both of my sons will decide to head back home and work towards building their father's dream of establishing a nationwide pharmacy chain that would compare with the best in the world.

MANAGE YOUR CASH CAREFULLY

If you fail to satisfy a customer and lose that customer's business, you can always work harder to please the next customer.

But if you fail to have enough cash to pay your suppliers, creditors, or your employees, you're out of business!

—Anonymous

Retail businesses are primarily cash businesses and this cash needs to be managed well and carefully. Daily cash reconciliation is critical in ensuring that the sale proceeds of the company are being banked correctly and on time every day.

Good cash management means knowing when, where and how your cash needs will occur, knowing what the best sources are for meeting additional requirements and being prepared to meet these when they occur. Keeping a close eye on cash flow is a key role that every entrepreneur has to play on a daily basis. In our early days, whenever I took my eyes off the cash flow we ran into trouble, either because daily cash reconciliation was not done or because payments were made indiscriminately and without prioritization.

Every Rupee Has to Be Collected and Counted

As we started to roll out stores, I realized how critical managing every rupee of sales was for the company.

In the early days, when we had a few stores, we had set up a simple 'cash drop box' in my house. At the end of the day, the staff who closed the store for the night would put all the cash collections into an envelope, come to my house and put this into the box. In order to ensure a second cheque, we had a register at home where each staff member would write down the amount of cash being deposited. This would be counter-signed by our cook or our housekeeper.

The next morning, one of the accounting clerks would open the locked box and deposit the money in the company's bank account. My staff at home got so involved in the process that I would hear our housekeeper asking the store personnel on some evenings why the sales were lower than the previous day. She had started to see a trend in the sales pattern! This process of cash collection lasted till we had eight stores, after which Vera put her foot down since she did not want to keep so much cash at home.

In addition to depositing the cash every night, the staff would also leave the store keys at our house and the following day, the morning shift staff would collect the keys to open the store.

The stated company policy on cash received from sales proceeds was very clear—every rupee of the sales proceeds was required to be deposited every day in the company bank account. The funds, after depositing, would get transferred into the common account through the banking system on a daily basis.

The store staff in our early days had a tendency to use the 'till' money from daily sales for reimbursements or for small petty expenses. This was completely unacceptable as per company policy, since using cash sale proceeds for expenses used to throw the daily reconciliation out of gear. Enforcing this discipline was a huge challenge and I can recall the numerous calls I made to the staff instructing, requesting and cajoling them to ensure cash collections were deposited every single day.

Personal Cash Flows Will Suffer

As a professional manager, I had never understood the meaning of the words, 'I am tight for cash.'

Throughout my professional career, I ensured that there was always sufficient money in the bank and, in any case, the next salary cheque would arrive at the end of every month. I would never think twice about incurring an expense; in fact, Vera always said that I was a compulsive spender. She would make up by saving money. Credit card bills used to be paid on the day the bill was received. I must have been a bad account for my credit card companies since they never earned any interest due to delayed payments from my account!

As I started my entrepreneurial journey, I did not draw a salary for the first thirty-six months, till 1 April 2006. While I thought I was making a sacrifice, I should not have done this. Every entrepreneur makes a lot of sacrifices, but one should not cut back on one's personal salary, since this sacrifice affects the well-being of the family.

This was a period when my expenses were high since my sons were in college, my free cash was being invested in my company and I had no cash flow coming in every month. I remember several instances of holding back on personal purchases. When a person goes into cost-cutting mode, every expense seems to be a waste—from electricity in the home to purchasing a shirt to eating out at restaurants to gifts for weddings and so on. I went through a similar process as I started to cut back dramatically on personal expenses.

This period was also the only time in my entire life when I delayed credit card payments and paid interest on them to manage my cash flow better.

Ensure Salary Payment to Employees on Time

Given my own background as a salaried employee for almost twenty-five years, I was clear that salary payments to staff on the seventh day of every month—or a day earlier if the seventh happened to be a Sunday or a holiday—was sacrosanct.

I was acutely aware of every individual's need to pay rents, school fees, equated monthly instalments and other monthly bills. I used to be surprised to hear from people that their salaries had been delayed or that the company owed them a few months of unpaid wages. How could any employer not pay his staff members their monthly wages? They had worked during the month and their monthly wages were theirs by right.

Cash flow in our early days was often tight and the funds in the company's bank account were often not enough to pay salaries. When we were faced with such tight positions, I used to move funds from my personal bank account to the company account to ensure that salaries were paid on time. Guardian has never delayed salary payments from the day we started operations and I know this is a source of pride and satisfaction for me and all my colleagues.

Remember to Set Your Own Compensation

Most entrepreneurs who want to build large businesses and create institutions tend to overlook their own compensation package, in the belief that since the company is 'their own', they should first build the organization before adding additional costs. This is an entrepreneur's way of saying that he is trying to conserve cash by not spending anything on himself. It is a big mistake that most entrepreneurs make—I was no different. No entrepreneur should undersell his own capability.

As I brought in external shareholders and then private equity funds, I realized that no one appreciated the so-called sacrifice that I thought I had made for the company. When I pointed this out at board meetings, I was simply told by the private equity investors, 'Why didn't you take a salary? We did not ask you not to compensate yourself.'

Suppliers Are Your Partners—Be Transparent with Them

As a company grows, cash flow is always tight and therefore, prioritizing cash payments is necessary. Money to meet monthly salaries, rental, utilities and communication bills have to be provided for every month without fail. I remember many meetings with my finance head, trying to figure out which supplier to pay and when and how to prioritize payments, so that the supplies would not suffer and the suppliers would be happy.

Using supplier funds is a common practice in most businesses and most suppliers know this. I realized that it is very important to carry our suppliers with us. They knew that delayed payments did not mean that their money was not safe—they simply wanted a confirmation of the delay so that they could plan their cash flows better. Each time payments were delayed from Guardian, the rumour mills would start working overtime and I would start getting feedback that our suppliers were nervous because they had heard that the company was closing down or that I had sold it off.

The number of times I was reported to have resigned or sacked by the board of the company or have sold off my stake would have made anyone nervous. During one extended visit overseas, the rumour mills started to suggest that I had run away. All these stories were started by disgruntled employees or people who had a strong interest in seeing us fail because their business was being affected by our stores.

In order to reinforce our suppliers' confidence, I have had many meetings with them in our offices and explained to them that the company was growing fast, but their payments would be delayed for the next few weeks. Every supplier has always supported us wholeheartedly throughout our journey.

On the other hand, distributors of some of the big brand fast-moving consumer goods companies simply would not accept any payment delays because they knew that the consumer demanded their products from our stores. We needed these distributors and suppliers more than they needed us, so we made sure we never delayed their payments.

Whenever we delayed payments too much (and this did happen several times) a few suppliers would stop providing goods. But the moment we would start ordering from another supplier, I would receive a complaint from them stating that we had stopped buying from them and their business with us was going down!

They understandably wanted payments on time, but they did not want to stop business with us—a clear indication to me that they trusted Guardian, they trusted our business and most importantly, they trusted our dream.

KEEP A VERY TIGHT CONTROL ON YOUR COSTS

Cost control must become a culture within the company and must start from the top.
Spending money is very easy, cutting back is very difficult.

Cost control has to start at the very top.

Nothing hurts more than when you see someone misusing your hard-earned money. Yet, as an entrepreneur, you have no choice but to accept this reality. An organization cannot have one set of rules for the promoter, a different set of rules for the senior management and another set for the remaining staff. I have never attempted to implement any rule in Guardian that I would not be willing to follow myself.

Even today, at the end of the day, I walk around the office switching off lights and air conditioners. During a visit to a store in peak winter when the temperature outside was 15°C, I was surprised to find the air conditioner switched on and the store door left open. When I asked the store in-charge why he had the door open and the air conditioner switched on, his response was, 'It was getting very cold inside the store so we thought we would open the door.'

Immediately thereafter, we put in place a policy to switch on air conditioners after Holi, in March, and switch off air conditioners after Diwali, in October–November.

I particularly remember a meeting in Shanghai with my friend T.T. Lim, former president of Walmart China, and now a very successful businessman. When TT came to meet me at the Grand Hyatt, Shanghai, he asked me a question, 'Who is paying for the hotel room?' I replied that I was. He responded with a smile and said, 'Looks like you have a lot of money to burn, especially when it is your own.'

I asked him to move me to the hotel that he normally stayed in after he had started off on his own. I shifted to a chain of hotels called Home Inns, which charged only twenty-five dollars a night. This chain was started by a local businessman and within fifteen years he had built over one hundred hotels across the country and got a valuation of over two billion dollars when he listed on NASDAQ.

This hotel provides very basic rooms with a clean bed, clean attached toilet, colour television, hot and cold water dispenser for tea and coffee, free Internet and free breakfast—all this for twenty-five dollars. This is all that a business traveller needs when he returns at the end of a long, hard day. In addition, the owner very smartly managed to get leading coffee chains to co-locate with his hotels and provided an entrance from the hotel lobby to the coffee shop. I now stay at a Home Inns hotel each time I visit China and have directed dozens of my Indian friends to this chain as well.

Costs in most new companies have this incredible ability to 'run away'. Before one realizes the impact, the bills have started coming in and these are difficult to stop. As a business grows, it becomes more difficult to control costs without hurting people. It is very easy to build overheads, very difficult to control them.

Phone and Internet

Telephone bills are always a very sensitive subject in most companies. Communication is every person's right and yet it can become a costly proposition for the organization, particularly for a retail company, because of the large number of calls involved between people and stores.

In order to expedite the opening of new stores, I had sanctioned the installation of a few wireless phones at the new stores, pending the installation of the regular fixed line phones. A few years later when I was reviewing telephone costs, I was surprised to find that someone in the administration department had made this a standard operating procedure, so that every new store was being issued a fixed wireless phone in addition to the regular landlines. Due to this we had over five hundred phones in the company that were not being used, but for which we were paying fixed monthly bills. Giving up so many phones became a challenge for us, as well as the phone company. It is possible that some young executive lost his job in the phone company for 'losing' the Guardian account.

The same issue applies to Internet costs, where the unit cost per MB of download is small, but when the total numbers of the company are considered, it becomes staggering. We have implemented a rule in our company according to which surfing the net and visiting unauthorized sites is prohibited.

Travel

Travel costs also have a habit of 'flying away'. These are easily justifiable by every manager since travel is needed to run the business and to meet the budgets. It took me time to explain to people that travel costs could be a large expense head and they needed to be managed. A number of senior managers find it 'awkward' to tell their subordinates about cutting back on expenses. What I have found even more surprising is that senior managers approve travel expense claims of subordinates without even looking at them. To this day, I have never understood whether they are participating in a popularity contest or feel awkward to ask questions or simply do not care about the company's money.

Setting in place norms for class of travel and hotel entitlements proved to be a big challenge for us, but once we had established the rules, my colleagues accepted them immediately.

Paper Bags

When we started designing packaging, my brief to our designer was that I wanted 'good, environment-friendly packaging' and not 'cheap stuff'. I had to pay for this later!

In my desire to make good carry bags, we created large paper bags at a cost of ₹16 per bag, a small paper bag at a cost of ₹10 per bag and a specially designed single strip medicine packet with a flap, at a cost of ₹4 per unit.

Once the first store opened, we realized that we were using a very expensive packet to deliver a single medicine strip. All our packaging was very expensive. We ran out of the smaller bags very quickly since we had not anticipated the demand properly. To make matters worse, we started giving a single strip of medicine worth ₹5 in a large paper bag worth ₹16. The revenue from the sale of the product was lower than the cost of the paper bag. The margin was even lower.

Further, the large paper bags became an instant hit with customers, who started asking for two extra bags with each purchase. If the store personnel said no, we would have an unhappy customer walking out of the door, so more often than not, they gave away free paper bags each time a customer asked for one. We must have given away thousands of non-revenue earning paper bags in our early days, costing us a small fortune.

Finally, our staff started using this paper bag for carrying lunch!

We changed to cheaper plastic bags soon thereafter. A number of environmentally aware customers did send us mails questioning the wisdom of moving to plastic from paper. We were not able to tell them that the reason was pure economics. When the government of Delhi came out with the legislation to stop using plastic bags, we were the first retail company to move back to paper (though much cheaper this time around) bags.

Bills

As we started to roll out more stores, a friend called me and asked why we were being an 'environment unfriendly company' and wasting so much paper in our bills.

According to the law, we are required to make two invoice copies—one for the customer, one for the store records. Since the Drugs and Cosmetics Act does not recognize computerized bills, we have to store the paper bills for at least eight years. At the end of each day, the licensed pharmacist is required to initial every bill every day. A computer-generated bill without the initial of the registered pharmacist could lead to a suspension of the store licence for a period of three days!

On checking, I found that our standard bill length was about fifteen inches and that a lot of paper was being wasted simply because we were leaving too much space between every line. I did a quick calculation and found that we were using over 5,000 kilometres of paper rolls in one year! We re-engineered the bill and reduced the length to six inches from the earlier fifteen inches (without removing any data that was required to be printed). Thus, we saved over 3,000 miles of paper rolls every year.

Similarly, we found that printer cartridges are a huge cost for a retail company. Every store has at least one printer while the regional offices and the head office have dozens of them. When we found out the huge cost involved in replacing so many cartridges, we took a decision to start refilling printer cartridges, saving the company lakhs of rupees every year.

Printer Paper

Another cost that I found running out of control was that of the paper used in printers and photocopiers.

Employees would print anything they wanted through one of several printers spread throughout the office floor, and I would often find hundreds of sheets of waste paper lying next to the printer in the morning. Someone would give a print command and not even bother to pick up the printout. All these printouts were single-sided prints, leading to a doubling of the costs, more so when it was unnecessary.

I found the same practice being followed at the photocopying machine, where a lot of documents would be sent for copying and then extra copies would be left lying around. Employees were also misusing the photocopier by copying personal books, which ran into several hundred pages. Other than the cost of the paper and being environmentally unacceptable, this was a serious data security lapse.

We implemented the following steps immediately to bring our costs under control:

- We earmarked a specific printer for a group of departments to identify who was wasting paper.
- We configured a default option on every computer to print on both sides of the paper.
- Using the code feature in the photocopier, we assigned a code to each department. Every person had to enter this code before they could operate the machine, and records were available for a scrutiny if necessary.

These were simple but very effective steps. We saved a lot of money by reducing paper wastage and brought in much greater accountability.

Security Guards

We have outsourced the security function in our company. When we decided to renew our contract, I was surprised to find that we were approached by senior retired defence and police officers who had set up their own security companies. We were looking for two hundred guards. The numbers were large and the cost was huge.

While talking to a customer, I overheard an interesting conversation. An old lady walked up to our guard and asked, 'Can you let me know where I can buy medicines?'

Without thinking, the guard pointed to the chemist next door and said, 'Go there.'

Our security guard did not even think, or possibly he just did not understand, that he was working as a security guard at a chemist shop!

These security guards are overworked and underpaid. The contractor takes the full payment from the company and passes on a small share to the guards, which is why the quality of work is generally below average. Since they are underpaid, some of them collude with store staff in pilfering goods, or in some cases they get together with a few individuals who pose as customers and come to steal goods from our stores.

I decided to withdraw all two hundred guards. They were of no use in protecting the assets inside the store. I am sure that we made the security consultants very unhappy.

Couriers

Another cost that I found rising exponentially was that of couriers. In most companies the administrative department is responsible for this cost, but has very little control over it since each department of the company individually sends couriers through the courier company.

At one stage, I realized to my horror that the then supply chain head had taken the easy way out and was sending all goods using a courier. We had paid to ship over one hundred kilograms of medicines and wellness products by courier to a new store we were opening in Bangalore simply because one individual decided that he did not want to be bothered by the cost and did not want to take the trouble of looking at surface transport options.

We established the norms and authorizations levels for courier costs soon after this and brought it under control.

Drinking Water

I was surprised to find one day, while reviewing our expenses, that the costs of mineral water had increased significantly and comprised around 1 per cent of the total costs of the office. On checking, I realized that we were ordering bottled water, which was being used not only for drinking but also for washing dishes in the cafeteria.

In addition, sometimes I would see some guards filling up water bottles for people walking past the building from our bottles. Once there was a line of people standing outside because one benevolent guard had decided to quench the thirst of many parched throats!

Cutting back on drinking water costs was bound to be misinterpreted. The first reaction that went around the office was that in my drive to scale down expenses, the company, and more particularly I, was not willing to provide drinking water to the employees.

We installed a reverse osmosis water purifier. While initially there was a lot of resistance, everyone came around when they realized that the entire senior management, including me, was also going to be drinking the same water.

Office Building

Most entrepreneurs tend to spend a lot of money in designing and renovating their offices. This expense, for all practical purposes, is 'dead' and will not give you any direct return, unless, of course, you are in a business where you wish to make an impression on your customers. Getting a fancy office with outstanding interiors does a lot for one's ego, but when the bills start to pile up, one wonders if the investment was a wise one.

I have consistently maintained that the only visitors to a retail company's head office are investors, potential investors, auditors and suppliers. Investors are always unhappy to see profligate spending on the head office of any company. Potential investors are happy if the company is careful with its money and keeps its overheads low. Suppliers don't care how much money a company spends as long as they get the business!

Therefore, the head office must be functional, clean and comfortable. At Guardian, we believe that we should spend our money on our stores, where our customers see us, instead of the head office, where our visitors don't really care.

I started my first office from my house and moved to a one-room sharing apartment. As we started to grow, we moved again, to a residential building where we had our offices in the basement and our conference room on the second floor. The ladies' toilet was on the third floor but none of the female staff ever complained.

Two years later, we moved again, this time into 3,000 square feet of space in a market square in central Gurgaon. As our office and warehouse space requirements increased, we gradually kept taking additional space till we had four offices in three locations in the same market square. This was becoming very inefficient, since we were multiplying all our administrative requirements four times. We were spending a lot of money in just sending office boys from one building to another. Setting up a telephone exchange and drawing wires from one office to another also became a huge challenge with the local authorities.

Thereafter, in June 2007, we moved further away from central Gurgaon and took a large office with 28,000 square feet of space. We moved our warehouse there as well. Moving out of the city centre meant that we were able to get a much larger area at a monthly rental lower than what we were paying in the market square. I christened this building 'Guardian House'.

I have always been a great believer in open offices or, if there are rooms, in having clear glass windows and doors. This brings a sense of informality in the office and the work atmosphere becomes much more open. I tell all my colleagues that there is nothing to hide in our company and, therefore, no need to hide behind any closed doors or partitions or blinds. This applies to my room as well.

A company-owned office building goes a long way in giving comfort to the staff that the company they work for is solid, stable and rooted. A few years after we started the company, we acquired land to construct a company-owned corporate office. We will in the next few years build our corporate office on this land.

This will be the culmination of a long journey to build Guardian, which started out from my house.

Cafeteria

When we moved to the larger office premises, the first thing we built after completing our office cubicles was a simple air-cooled cafeteria. We asked one of our suppliers to donate plastic chairs and tables and outsourced the canteen kitchen to a local vendor.

Every day, the entire office, from the junior-most to the senior-most employee, uses the same cafeteria for lunch. Most of us bring our own food and share each other's lunches. Every table has a mini buffet set up and I know that all my colleagues look forward to their lunch break. The Guardian cafeteria is well known for its excellent stuffed parathas. On weekdays, very often, some of my friends stop by at lunch to eat parathas with me. Not a very healthy snack from a wellness company!

Office Equipment

Simple office equipment like a heavy-duty photocopier and overhead projector in the conference room are essential requirements. These facilities are generally rented by most companies.

The cost of acquiring these assets, particularly a photo-copying machine, is very low. Running outside for a simple photocopy is extremely inconvenient. Work gets delayed and tempers are frayed simply because a paper sent for photocopying has not been brought back for over an hour.

Every office must also have a basic paper shredder. I have found our store revenue, purchase margin and salary printouts reaching our competition simply because someone forgot to destroy old copies of these important documents and left them lying around.

We invested in all the basic office equipment to make the lives of the office staff as comfortable as possible.

Generator

We spend over ten hours a day in our offices, so uninterrupted supply of electricity is essential. Most small buildings under-provide generating capacity in the mistaken belief that they are saving money, but end up paying much more because of larger running costs and through many hours of lost productivity. A generator is the last expense that should be saved or cut back on, assuming that it is being managed properly and the diesel used for the generator is stored in an area from where it cannot easily be stolen.

At Guardian, we planned for excess generator capacity to ensure that all our air conditioners should be able to run on internally generated power.

Company Vehicles

Company-owned vehicles, be it cars, trucks, vans or two-wheelers, are always an expensive proposition.

When we started out, we purchased a few vans and a

number of scooters for home delivery. Within a few months, I found that all vehicles had started giving trouble. The fuel consumption pattern went haywire and if a delivery scooter was expected to give at least forty kilometres per litre, we started getting bills showing forty kilometers for every five litres. New tyres would wear out within three months and each time a driver would be questioned, he would look at us with his most innocent expression and say, 'I have no idea how this has happened.'

As we kept delivery scooters at all stores, the costs started to escalate exponentially. Boxes fixed behind the scooter were broken and to make matters worse, we were once fined by the traffic police for a badly kept scooter. That particular vehicle was not even one year old.

We found that our vans were running up large bills on maintenance and fuel. Thereafter we outsourced the vans to a third party and found that our supplies to stores became completely unreliable. We then came back to owning our own vans and the original problems surfaced once again.

Our vans would get caught by the police on some small pretext at various state borders quite often, resulting in delayed supplies on the one hand and unnecessary costs to get our vans released on the other. Coupled with this was the problem of the drivers taking leave, I remember one driver who had given a leave application on account of his grandmother's death three times!

We decided to change the entire system and sold all our vans and scooters. We outsourced deliveries of our goods from the warehouse to the stores to a local contractor and though the initial cost was higher, we started to see significant savings because we had no recurring costs and no drivers' moods to deal with.

We did the same thing for two-wheelers, except that we fixed a rate per kilometre for the two-wheelers used on company work and asked store staff to use their own scooters and motorcycles for home delivery. We were careful to factor in the cost of fuel and the wear and tear of the vehicle into the cost per kilometre that we agreed to reimburse. The delivery boys resented this initially, since they thought that a perquisite had been taken away from them. Later, when they started to see that they would actually save money by using their own vehicle and in a number of cases even make money, they willingly accepted the proposition.

Company Movable Assets

I have seen—both when I was a professional manager and in my life as an entrepreneur—how company assets are generally misused.

As explained in the previous section, I took a call right from the beginning that Guardian would not provide any company-owned cars or two-wheelers to employees and that the cost of this perquisite would be built into the total package of each employee. We decided to add a fixed amount to the salary package so that the employee could own his car, rather than provide them a company-owned car or scooter.

I could not follow the same practice for the other company-owned assets, though. Many a time I have found store air conditioners damaged within a few months of installation, computer keyboards with tea or coffee spilt on them, a new mobile handset with a damaged screen or broken chairs. In such cases I ask my colleagues if they don't replace the compressor of the air conditioner in their homes within six months, or if their home computer has any dust, leave alone tea, on it.

For some strange reason, employees show no respect for company-owned assets. However, if these assets belong to them or if they think that after a few years they can purchase the same for themselves at a depreciated price, then the asset's life increases and maintenance quality improves.

We have just launched an 'own your notebook computer' scheme where we have told all employees that the company would subsidise the purchase of their notebooks by 50 per cent. This subsidy would be available to all employees every three years, implying that they would be able to buy a new computer every three years. Suddenly I see employees cleaning their notebooks very carefully!

We don't have any more broken screens, damaged computer hinges, noisy fans, burnt mother boards, lost chargers or batteries that need replacement within six months. Employees now have 'more skin in the asset' and hence maintenance and longevity of the assets have improved.

GUARDIAN BRANDS

Buy Smart Buy Guardian
Why Pay More

The name 'private label' or 'white label' derives from the white label on a product's packaging, which can be filled in with the marketer's trade address. Its origins can be traced back to the time of vinyl records, when DJs would remove the label from a popular record so that other DJs would not know who made the track. Doing this would create what was known as a 'white label' record.

At Guardian, we decided that it was an essential part of our strategy to build a full range of Guardian-branded products to compete with the well-established brands that we sold in our stores, and to offer a strong value proposition at a lower cost offering an economical choice to our customers. We also needed our private label brands to increase our margins and to increase footfall by bringing repeat customers back to our stores because of the quality of the products under our brand.

Guiding Principles for Guardian Brands

Before we placed our first set of orders for our brands, we decided to outline the broad principles under which we would operate:

- We would ensure that all our products would match or exceed the quality standards of the best in the industry. There would be no compromise on the quality.
- We would not attempt any product that required new research or huge investments in creating consumer awareness.
- The packaging of the product would be the best in its class.
- We would price the product at a level at least 25 per cent lower than the top two competitors in its category.
- We would only consider products that had a minimum margin of 50 per cent.
- We would not enter any category that was dominated by a single player controlling over 75 per cent of the market share in its category.
- We would only enter those areas where the products were fast-moving and where we believed that customer loyalty could be shifted because of the value the customer saw in our product.
- We would create products that would generally have a year-round sale. We would not invest in products that could be sold only during one season or a few months of the year.
- We would build all products to leverage the credibility of the Guardian brand.

Thereafter, based on a lot of primary research inside stores of global pharmacy chains as well as a significant amount of secondary research on the Internet, we identified twelve broad categories.

Once these categories had been frozen, we worked on the subcategories, the products and the SKUs. Looking at our needs a few years down the line, I established the norms for the code numbers for each category, subcategory, product and SKU.

Every private label was given a nine digit code, which was allocated as follows:

- Two digits for Guardian private labels
- Two digits for the category
- Two digits for the subcategory
- Two digits for the product
- One digit for the SKU

I decided that the inclusion of any new category could only be done after my written approval. In addition, we agreed that the approval of the pricing of all products would need a final signoff from me. Other than these two requirements that I insisted upon, my colleagues had the flexibility to develop and launch any product.

Over the last eighteen months, we have launched over 250 SKUs of Guardian-branded private labels, which have been very well received in the marketplace; and in each category the Guardian private label brand has a share of at least 15 per cent. Customers have started to get used to some of the Guardian-branded products and have made these their preferred choice. We are constantly reviewing our products and are in regular touch with suppliers to improve the quality and lower the prices.

Logo

We had already decided internally that all our private label brands would come from the 'House of Guardian'.

Instead of simply using the word Guardian as we had done for our store brand, I wanted to do something different for our private label products. While I wanted to use the Guardian name, I did not wish to repeat the font or stylized design of the pharmacy, nor did I want to put the cross on the private label packaging.

While brainstorming with one of my board members and shareholders, he came up with the brilliant yet simple idea that we should pull out the little angel from inside our cross and replace the letter 'I' in Guardian with 'Y'. We also changed the font into a bolder lettering to emphasize the brand name. Then we standardized a narrow blue stripe at the bottom of the brand name, which would mention the descriptor of the category. This single unit now became the brand identifier that would be placed on every single Guardian-branded private label.

We tried this out and it was instantly liked by everyone. The brand name was still Guardian, yet its look and feel created the differentiation I was looking for.

'Buy Smart Buy Guardian/Why Pay More'

Based on the guiding principles for our brands, we took a decision that our positioning platform for all Guardian brands would be 'value for money'. I worked with our advertising agency to develop the tag line for our brands which said, 'Buy Smart Buy Guardian/Why Pay More'

Category Names

When we started naming the product categories, the easiest and most obvious option that we could have taken was to use Guardian. However, I wanted to create two or three separate brand families, one for our pharmaceutical products and one for our OTC, nutrition and beauty products.

We decided to use the words 'Xtra' as a prefix for the OTC, nutrition and beauty products and 'Guard' as a suffix for pharmaceutical products in most of our private label brands.

In addition, we used 'Guardian' as a house brand with generic product descriptors such as Ayurveda juices and diapers.

We do have products which do not conform to this, but these are exceptions and will be rechristened when the next round of ordering takes place.

After a lot of experimentation, we decided that we would consolidate our brand categories under the following heads:

- XtraCare for personal care products
- XtraVeda for Ayurveda products
- XtraVital for vitamin products
- XtraMuscle for sports nutrition products
- XtraVigour for vitality products
- XtrAqua for mineral water
- XtraSlim for weightloss products

In addition we decided to use the suffix 'Guard' for all our generic medicines. For example, we named our paracetamol 'ParaGuard' and our Azithromycin antibiotic tablet 'AziGuard'. Both these brands have been well accepted by doctors and customers.

We have two more names that we will use either as a prefix or a suffix so that in the next few years, we will have four strong brand families in addition to the mother 'Guardian' brand.

Goods Manufactured in China

Our first private labels were manufactured in China. In order to get acquainted with the manufacturers there, I first floated multiple enquiries on Alibaba.com. I was amazed to see the response. An enquiry to manufacture baby diapers got us over one hundred responses from manufacturers listed on the website.

Once I had a broad idea of what I could expect to buy from China, I decided to participate as a buyer in the Canton Trade Fair in Guangzhou. This is the largest trade fair I have ever seen and is held twice a year in April and October. Every manufacturer of any consequence from China and every serious buyer from all over the world makes it a point to attend this fair. At the end of the first day, I must have walked over ten miles through the aisles of the one hall which was relevant to me (there were at least six such halls). I collected over twenty kilograms of brochures on the first day.

The following day, I took a small suitcase with wheels to collect more brochures. What amazed me was that virtually every manufacturer at this fair claimed to be a supplier to most of the global pharmacy chains and they were even able to show photocopies of orders they had received.

During a visit to Xiamen in the southeast part of China, I travelled into remote parts of the country to visit a manufacturer of diapers and sanitary napkins. Soon we started importing container-loads of Guardian-branded products from this manufacturer.

My learnings in sourcing from China, especially as the founder of a small company that was beginning to grow, have been:

- Talk to at least six suppliers before you take a decision on who to source from. You will be surprised at the significant price differential.
- Do not get taken in by the certificates from major buyers that most manufacturers will show you. If you have contacts with any of these buyers, do a quick reference check on your chosen manufacturers.
- Negotiate long and hard. Keep walking away from the

deal and the supplier will keep calling you back. When you reach a price that is unacceptable, he will not call you back. This is when you know that you have reached his lowest bargaining position. Use this price to close the deal with the next manufacturer.

- Some businessmen will pretend not to speak English, though they are fluent in it. They will never speak to one another in any language other than Mandarin. Give yourself an advantage as well and talk in Hindi or your local language with your colleagues in front of them.

- Never put all your cards on the table with a manufacturer. He will spring many surprises in the negotiation and therefore you must be well armed with your own set of curveballs.

- The moment you show the slightest weakness to your supplier, you would have lost the advantage.

- The only hold a buyer has on a manufacturer is money for the current shipment. I have seldom come across a manufacturer who is willing to invest for the long term in a buyer–seller relationship.

- You must never expect to receive any settlement for damaged or substandard goods. You will always be given a plausible excuse that you have no choice but to accept.

- Agree on your pack designs and quality standards in writing, ask for a test pack for approval once you open your letter of credit and before you give your go-ahead to manufacture.

- Ensure that you conduct a pre-shipment quality examination before the goods leave the factory. You will never be able to recover a claim for faulty goods later.

- Always ask your supplier to deliver your goods to your nominated clearing and forwarding agent at your designated port in China. Don't ask for delivery to India. A Chinese manufacturer has no interest in the goods once he has shipped them out of his factory. The moment the export shipment leaves his factory gate, he shall cash your letter of credit and move on to the next order.

Goods Manufactured in India

Most of the Guardian brands are now being sourced from Indian manufacturers. We have excellent manufacturing facilities in India, but our processes and practices leave a lot to be desired.

Substandard quality, poor packaging, short supplies against order, nonconformity to delivery schedules and poor or incorrect documentation of the goods supplied appear to be the rule rather than the exception. Advance money is always demanded, but should normally not be given because once an advance has been given, there will be no guarantee that the supply will be made within the stipulated timeframe.

It is also critical to ensure that your documentation is done properly to address road permits and interstate taxes for all supplies from Indian manufacturers. If the documents have even the smallest error, the delivery truck can get held up at state borders, leading to unnecessary and unplanned delays.

However, we have now learned how to ensure we get the right quality and if this does not happen, how to get our money back!

In all my travels around the world I have noticed that it is very difficult to get a Chinese businessman to say 'yes' and it is equally difficult to get an Indian businessman to say 'no'! 'Jugaad' is the buzzword for most Indian businessmen and as a buyer, one needs to be careful to ensure that one is getting what one has contracted to buy.

Our search for new products to be manufactured under our brand continues relentlessly. We constantly keep talking to potential suppliers across the country and visiting trade fairs in different parts of Asia to expand our range of products with better packaging at lower prices. We aim to add at least fifty new SKUs every year to the stable of Guardian Brands.

BUILD, CONSOLIDATE, GROW–
CHALLENGES OF GROWTH

*...everyone wants to live on top of the mountain, but all
the happiness and growth occurs while you're climbing it.*

—Andy Rooney, radio and TV personality

I believe there are three stages in the life cycle of any new
company: build, consolidate, grow.

In the first stage, we managed to build two hundred stores
through the sheer brute strength of the people of Guardian, as
everyone put their shoulders to the wheel and pushed in the
same direction.

In the second stage, the next three hundred stores will be
built with a lot of pain, since we will be forced to introduce
strong systems and all of us will have to inculcate a strong
sense of self-discipline.

In the third stage, once we cross five hundred stores, the
systems we are now building will be strong enough to manage the
daily problems faced by startups. The role of senior management
will change once again to guiding the company through
uncharted waters as they expand in multiple geographies. For
this they will need to keep a strong hand on the rudder.

As the Guardian chain continued to grow, we found that
continuous growth is not necessarily a very wise thing to

achieve. Every company and every management team needs to stop, take a breath, take stock and consolidate operations before they start to expand the company once again.

Some of the areas that every entrepreneur who is rapidly expanding his business must consider are:

Systems

The first area where I started noticing problems was in our systems. When rapid growth takes place, managers tend to cut corners and take shortcuts. This always has long-term implications on the organization, but in the short term, the concerned manager is able to 'show' that he has met his immediate targets. Some of the areas where I found managers had taken shortcuts that had a direct implication on the operations if the company were:

Operations: With so much pressure to open stores and lack of trained staff, our operations leadership was forced to keep moving people from one store to another. This led to a significant increase in pilferage of stocks, since store staff realized very quickly that no one was watching them and frequent movement from one store to another gave them the protection of pilfering stocks and moving on before being found out.

Projects: We have a standard store-opening checklist, which outlines every step that has to be completed before a store is opened. With pressure to build more stores, the project excutives stopped following the laid-down procedures. Non-completion of all the items on the checklist as a result of suboptimal opening of stores was another casualty.

Quality: Since the contractors who were building the stores were under pressure to complete the stores quickly, they started using substandard material on the walls and on the floors. This resulted in entire shelves coming off the walls where they were grouted after the store had opened, resulting in a loss of stocks.

People: Our need for people was substantial since we were opening more than five stores a month. We had walk-in interviews going on in our head office. Our process of putting every new entrant through one week of training had to be foregone. Instead of training people after hiring them, we started hiring them and immediately asking them to report at a store the following morning. Our customer service suffered and I started to get negative customer feedback.

Technology: While we have a robust IT system to manage our stores, we realized that some of our hardware had started giving trouble and therefore computerized bills could not be issued. Some stores started to use manual bill books when the computer in the store was not working. It was standard policy that all manual bills would be entered in the computer later to be 'regularized' on a daily basis. But our errant store staff did not do so. This resulted in lost sales and lost cash for the company because if a manual bill was not entered in the computer and disappeared later, there was no way to track what had happened to the stock unless it was physically counted.

Cash: Reconciliation of cash collections on a daily basis, which is sacrosanct for any retail company, was stopped because it was seen as too cumbersome. Our finance department had to go through very intensive work for over one month to get this reconciliation done prior to our audit.

Stocks: While my colleagues in the loss prevention department were mandated to conduct stock checks every quarter in every store, this schedule fell by the wayside and I found out later that more than nine months had elapsed without a physical stock check. When we did conduct the stock-taking exercise, we found stocks missing and the people who should have been held responsible for these stocks at the stores had resigned. The company, once again, had to absorb a loss that it should not have borne had systems been implemented correctly.

Handling the Authorities

Every business in India has to learn to address the 'authorities'. Without developing this ability, it will face innumerable road blocks in conducting normal business operations.

In the early days of any new company, these relationships have to be handled directly by the entrepreneur and as the company grows, more people have to be brought in at various levels to manage relationships. Transferring these relationships from the entrepreneur to his colleagues is also a huge challenge, since everyone wants to deal only with the entrepreneur and no one else.

From drug inspectors to the inspectors under the Weights and Measurements Act, from local policemen to the clerk at the interstate check point, from customs inspectors to the inspector who monitors deduction of provident funds, and from the local legislator to the local bureaucrat, everyone has to be managed and everyone's ego needs to be massaged.

We seem to have moved from the licence raj to inspector raj. Everyone has some authority and he makes it a point to let this be known. I found that in my entrepreneurial journey, a lot of my time was spent unproductively in managing some of these relationships.

Upgrading Your Skills

Every company which grows quickly has to accept frequent changes in its management, since better skills are needed to manage every stage of growth.

The Peter Principle, propounded by Dr Laurence J. Peter and Raymond Hullin in 1969, could not have been more appropriate for new companies: 'In a hierarchy every employee tends to rise to his highest level of incompetence.'

We have also gone through this process—a number of people have left us on their own and a number of them have been asked to leave. People who were outstanding at one stage of our growth may not necessarily be appropriate a few years later, because they have chosen not to grow their own skill sets.

The Peter Principle applies to an entrepreneur as well. He has to ensure that he stays ahead of the principle if he does not want to find himself redundant within his own organization. Continuous training and retraining is necessary for every entrepreneur to remain contemporary and to retain the ability to lead a team of newer, fresher and more agile minds.

Reviews

Reviewing performances on daily, weekly, monthly, quarterly and annual basis is necessary to set up a proper system of reporting within the organization. Most managers don't like reviews. It took me a while to get all of them to understand why I wanted reviews.

I wanted my managers to realize that they would be able to manage their own roles better when they had access to organized data given to them as per an agreed schedule, reporting against an agreed set of targets. Guardian now has a very comprehensive system of reporting, though I still believe that a number of managers are not making proper use of the reports.

Some of the reports we have implemented in the company are:

Daily sales report: Each store sends a daily report which gives a lot of data. The report shows the sales figures for the store for that day for the month and for the year. It also compares this data with the budget for the same period as well as compares the sales to the same period in the previous year This enables the store staff to see their store performance versus budget and as compared to the previous year.

Daily MIS (Management Information System): At the end of each day, the executive committee members get a set of reports generated by our information technology department which collates our daily sales by business heads and business verticals. They also contain daily margins and daily stocks.

Weekly meetings: Every Monday morning, the executive committee meets and reviews the performance of the company till the close of business on the previous Friday. We look at revenues, margins, discounts, inventories and the number of people who have joined or left.

Monthly reviews: At the end of every month, we review the numbers versus the budgets as well as the profit and loss of each store and each business vertical. These meetings also help us to plan better for the coming month and I have often seen healthy arguments between functional heads when one person feels that another department is not pulling its weight.

Monthly board reports: Every month, we send a detailed set of financials and store numbers to the board of directors of the company for their review and comments. These reports are also circulated to the members of the executive committee as they give a complete picture of the performance of the company for the month and where we stand versus our approved budgets.

Quarterly reviews: We conduct a detailed review with our board of directors every quarter where, in addition to looking at our financials, we also look at what went right and what went wrong. A quarterly interaction with the board of directors helps the management to understand the long-term perspective of the board.

Annual review: We hold an annual plan review at our fourth quarterly meeting. This is normally a two-day meeting with the board of directors where we review our performance for the entire year and present our plan for the forthcoming year. We seek the board's approval of the plan and their guidance on our strategy for the coming year. At the quarterly and annual reviews with the board, my role changes from functioning as the CEO of the company to the chairman of the board.

◆

Once the operations leadership was convinced about the reports, they instituted their own set of simpler reports on a daily basis. Each store in-charge now sends an SMS on the daily sales to his area manager at the close of the business day. The area manager summarizes these messages and sends an SMS to the business vertical head, who does the same to the chief operating officer. I generally get to know the sales for the previous day through this informal channel of reporting before the daily

MIS reaches me.

In addition, there are several reports that are generated by different departments on a regular basis to conduct their own reviews.

Every review we conduct helps us streamline our operations.

Controls

Ensuring control systems and adhering to the company's standard operating procedures has to become like a 'sixth sense' for people within an organization.

In well-established companies, why don't staff members take unauthorized leave or come to work late or leave without giving any notice? Why do startup companies have to accept a much higher threshold of indiscipline and compromise on their operating standards?

Implementing a culture of controls across the organization can generally be achieved through a carrot and stick approach.

Projects

The construction of new stores is the largest cash outflow for any retail company. This is also an area where there is likely to be significant 'leakage' of the company's resources because of unethical practices that creep in due to poor hiring.

We had to get rid of several people in our projects team because we found them compromising the interests of the company with landlords. One incident was of particular importance.

I had approved the signing of a lease at the rate of ₹100 per square foot per month and had asked my colleague to try and negotiate this down by another 5 per cent. This person came back a few days later and said that the landlord had increased the price by 10 per cent. Since I wanted the store, I asked him to go ahead.

When we signed the lease, it was signed at 20 per cent over the original price approved by me and was significantly higher than the market price of other stores in the same market. We realized that our employee was hand-in-glove with the landlord and had to ask him to leave the company.

Growth

We have gone through the exercise of building and consolidating every two years before we start growing again, and after a period of relative quiet in the year 2012, we have started to grow again in 2013 and 2014.

I am certain that the process of building, consolidating, reviewing and growing is a cycle that we will continue throughout the life of the company.

Growth Through Acquisition

Growth of a business through acquisition is always a good means to expand exponentially, but this comes with its own sets of challenges related to integrating management teams. In addition, there are always serious issues relating to the 'unknown factors' that a new business may suddenly present. Other than the above, the single biggest challenge in handling inventory is that there could be a lot of damaged and unsaleable stocks that come with the acquisition.

I have also looked at acquisition because this would give Guardian an opportunity to grow quickly. We have taken over businesses of individual chemists and integrated them into the Guardian network. In addition, we have also looked at some of the smaller retail chains, but have generally been confronted with the 'build versus buy' economics. So far we have always believed that it is cheaper to build a new store. However, the dynamics of the Indian pharmacy market is beginning to change.

Over the past decade several pharmacy chains have started and closed down. There are a few chains left and the opportunity to acquire and consolidate operations to build a large chain is a definite possibility now.

Networking

Building a business needs a lot of networking, since every entrepreneur needs to understand his environment and stay connected with the outside world to get new ideas. Entrepreneurs must recognize that there is a huge world 'beyond his dream'.

There are many professional organizations that can help an entrepreneur to network, the primary one among these being The Indus Entrepreneurs (TiE). I have been lucky to have been involved with some of the largest and most widely dispersed groups of professional managers, businessmen, government officials and leading thinkers.

Young Presidents' Organization (YPO) and World Presidents' Organization (WPO)

The Young Presidents' Organization is a global body, set up in 1954 with the objective of getting like-minded CEOs on a common platform since 'it is lonely at the top'. YPO members have always provided a strong support network for me and I have called upon them each time I needed any help or advice. I have made some of my closest friends through this network.

I was invited to join YPO by the Singapore chapter in

1994 and have been a member of this wonderful organization ever since. As I grew older, I graduated to the YPO's graduate organization—WPO, the World Presidents' Organization.

Global Alliance of Vaccines and Immunization (GAVI)

In November 2006, I was invited to join the board of the Global Alliance of Vaccines and Immunization (GAVI). GAVI was conceived at the World Economic Forum meeting in Davos in 2000, based on an initiative taken by Nelson Mandela and supported by Bill Gates. Its mission is to save children's lives and protect people's health by increasing access to immunization in poor countries. I have committed at least fifteen working days a year to GAVI because I believe in the cause. This organization has enabled me to understand the health systems in several countries

Stay Away from the Hype

After being burnt several times in my professional life, I have learnt that it is better to keep a low profile and 'stay under the radar' as the company grows. Whenever I have been asked why I don't appear in the press often enough or why Guardian is not seen more often in the media, my comment is always the same, 'Let my stores do the talking and let my customers be the judge.'

For me, the simple lesson while building your business is, 'Do not get carried away by your own hype!'

FRANCHISING–A GOOD WAY TO GROW

I have found no greater satisfaction than achieving success through honest dealing and strict adherence to the view that, for you to gain, those you deal with should gain as well.

—Alan Greenspan, economist

For most retail businesses, franchising offers an excellent opportunity for the brand to grow across a large geographical territory very quickly.

Opening up a company's systems and its heart to an individual who wants to come on board primarily because he senses a financial return on his investment takes an organization time to understand and digest. It is essential to ensure that a company embarks on franchising only when the organization and its people are ready to welcome a franchisee into its fold.

Benefits of Franchising

From the perspective of a franchisee, it is important to understand what benefits they can expect from the franchise and from the perspective of a franchisor, they must understand that they must be able to provide value to any potential franchisee.

Consumers buy from brands they trust: Brands convey credibility to a consumer and outlive any promoter or manager.

A strong brand ensures long-term profits and an association with a strong and credible franchisor helps build a sustainable business for an investor.

The franchisor must support his brand and the franchisee must assure the brand owner that the brand will be respected and that no steps would ever be taken that would tarnish its image or diminish its value.

Efficient business practices as systems are proven: Strong companies are able to bring foolproof systems and good business practices into the business of any franchisee. It is important to adhere to these values to ensure that there is no clash of values between the franchisor and the franchisee.

Marketing costs are lower through volume: Becoming a member of a large franchise operation helps to defray marketing costs over a large number of business owners.

Mentoring the franchisees: Guardian has put together a senior team that is available to mentor all franchisees through their early stages. This mentoring is really an extract of all the learnings of the company over a period of time through experience.

Reduced risk through proven business model: At Guardian, we believe that our learnings can be transferred to a potential franchisee so that his learning curve is not as steep or as expensive as ours has been.

Defined territories protect franchisees from competition: Once a franchise territory has been defined, it becomes a valuable piece of 'real estate', since there would be no other Guardian franchisee in this defined territory.

Franchisor Checklist

As a franchisor, we look at what we can offer to a potential franchisee before we agree to sign up and give the rights to our brand to any franchisee.

Strong value proposition: We believe that Guardian is slowly but surely growing into a strong pharmacy brand and therefore we are confident that we are now in a position to start accepting franchisees. Today, we believe we have a strong value proposition for any individual who takes a decision to take a Guardian franchise.

Control systems: We have built strong back-office and control systems to help a franchisee manage his business, as well for us to manage several franchisees.

Buy-in from everyone within the company: Getting a buy-in from every department and every head of department is essential for the process to work. At Guardian, we are beginning to create a dedicated team of people who will be able to address the issues faced by any franchisee.

Don't differentiate from company-owned store: Franchisee stores have the same needs as those of a company-owned store and the franchisor cannot afford to differentiate between these stores. This problem becomes more acute at the field level where issues start between the two formats. Such issues need to be tackled immediately before these become serious problems.

Who holds the lease on the property: We also like to check the title deeds of the property that is proposed to be converted into a Guardian store. We cannot afford to open a store at a location and then close this because of reasons other than those of pure business.

Franchisee Checklist

Before an individual takes up a franchise of any brand, I believe that he must address the following questions. Once money is committed, it becomes difficult to change one's mind.

Is this the right franchise for you: Every franchisee should ask himself whether he has the skills or the training to handle a pharmacy business. I have met a number of potential franchisees who assume that they simply have to make an investment and then wait for the results. When I tell them that they have to actually run their store, they start to think twice.

Get professional advice from an accountant, lawyer or other business expert: My colleagues and I always ask a potential franchisee to develop a business plan before they start making the investment. Unless a franchisee understands his own business model, he will never be able to extract the maximum value for his franchise in terms of monthly returns after meeting all his costs.

Guardian does not prepare or commit to a business plan for any franchisee. All that we do is to give the assumptions for preparing a business plan and share all the relevant data from a company-owned store of a similar size in a similar market. The business has to be run by the franchisee and they have to commit to their numbers, not us.

Check out the franchisor: We gave a detailed data pack on Guardian to every potential franchisee and we always ask him to conduct a detailed due diligence on the company and its directors. This is important so that a person who wants to invest money satisfies himself about the company and people behind the company.

Speak with existing franchisees: We also encourage potential franchisees to meet and discuss the Guardian experience with other franchisees only when they hear a satisfied franchisee speaking will they understand the value we can create for them as a brand and as an organization.

What is the exit strategy and what goodwill can be retained: For every potential franchisee, Guardian offers an exit by offering to buy out the franchise at the end of the agreed period. If the franchisee wishes to continue longer, we will renew the franchise on terms then applicable.

The Guardian Experience

When we first started the franchising process, we put together a package for potential franchisees, which included:

- The Guardian brand name
- Guardian systems
- Supply of all products
- Extra margins on supplies
- *Guardian Health Chronicle*
- GNC products
- Availability of Guardian brands

This package had not been thought through carefully and as an organization, we had not matured sufficiently to work with any franchisee.

We realized that we were not able to deliver goods to a franchisee on time, which resulted in a loss of credibility. We were also unable to deliver sufficient margins to these franchisees since they would go out into the market, buy goods and pay in cash, which would get them slightly higher margins. Our income from the franchisee was through a revenue share of the sales. The easiest way for the franchisee to avoid paying us was to not make a bill for the sales made. Several of our franchisees started to sell goods and did not prepare computerized bills. This resulted in the loss of our franchise fees on the sales.

A number of our franchisees took goods from us and did not bother to settle their dues, and quite a few of them gave us post-dated cheques for our fees, which would generally bounce. Bounced cheques and unrecovered dues for our supplies resulted in large write-offs for Guardian, which is when we stopped the franchising scheme.

Since the company was growing and there was a lot of pressure on top management from company-owned stores, franchisee stores were not getting the attention they deserved.

We stopped franchising and decided to regroup and re-launch when we were ready, and when we had a strong value proposition.

The Guardian Experience—2010

In early 2010, we sat down to reevaluate our position as a strong brand to franchise. I was certain that unless we could outline our strengths, we would not be able to convince any potential franchisee to invest in the Guardian brand.

We looked at the Guardian value proposition and realized that over the last three years, since we had stopped our unsuccessful franchise attempt, we had achieved the following:

- The Guardian brand, with its unique purple colour, was now well-respected in North India and was definitely the market leader in the National Capital Region.
- Our margins were amongst the highest in the industry and we had strong partnerships in place with manufacturers and other suppliers.
- Our private label portfolio was possibly the strongest in the country and we would be able to offer significantly higher margins to a franchisee.
- Our partnerships with GNC and Yves Rocher had led to unique products which were not available in any other pharmacy. These products also offered very attractive margins.
- Our systems had matured and were stable, and we had started to invest in upgrading them.
- Our management team was much stronger and was now ready, capable and willing to support a franchisee.
- Our investment in our newspaper, the *Guardian Health Chronicle*, over the past four years had built a strong customer following.
- Our electronic marketing capabilities had improved significantly and we were in a position to access at least 500,000 customers via email.
- Our loyalty programme, the Guardian XtraValu card, had over 350,000 members.
- Our supply chain was strong. However, we were only in a position to supply our own products and not third-party products to franchisees. We therefore decided that we would give a list of preferred vendors with agreed margins and payment terms to a franchisee rather than try and supply these goods ourselves—something we had failed to do earlier.

Based on our internal discussion and the evaluation report of our top management task force, we came to the conclusion that we were ready to franchise. We mandated the management team to verify every potential franchisee before any agreement was signed.

We decided that our terms would have to be followed to ensure that the franchisee succeeded, but removed all the areas where we knew we had created dissonance with the franchisees.

In the success of each of our franchisees lay our success. We therefore decided that:

- We would not compromise on our terms with the franchisees.
- We would not guarantee or commit to any revenues. We would assist the franchisee to develop his business plan but these numbers would be his numbers, not ours.
- We would not accept any part payment from the franchise as we had done in the past.
- We would not give any credit terms to the franchisee. If money was not received, goods would not leave our warehouse.
- We would insist on approving the store drawings and the interiors, but we would not insist on using any specific contractors.
- We would insist on using standard systems, but we would not take a percentage royalty each month from sales so that there would be no temptation to bill 'outside the system'.
- We would not supply third-party goods, but we would recommend suppliers from whom Guardian was getting the highest margins.
- We would insist on a mix of Guardian-branded products,

GNC products and Yves Rocher products being kept at each store since these brands provided the USP to a franchisee.

When we released our first advertisement inviting franchisees, we received over seventy-five applications. We started a number of new franchisees but once again the innovative schemes started by our franchisees to beat the systems were amazing. We soon realized that managing a franchisee was not something that we could do effectively.

After running the revised franchisee operation for a few years the board of the company decided that we would only open company-owned stores.

SUPPLY CHAIN—CHALLENGES

At P&G, we decided to stop being so company-centric, and start being customer-centric and demand-driven. We found when you do that, some amazing things happen.

—Ralph Drayer, former chief logistics officer at
Procter & Gamble

A few years ago, I was visiting the warehouse of GNC in North Carolina. This was a fully automated warehouse spread across over one million square feet and was one of three warehouses that serviced over 5,000 GNC stores across the length and breadth of America. The sheer size and scale of this warehouse was extremely intimidating and yet I knew that the people of GNC managed these warehouses with incredible efficiency and precision.

For every retail chain, the supply network is the heart of the company. Unless the supply chain pumps out life-giving products and the goods reach the stores in time, customers will not be able to get what they want from us and will return disappointed.

At Guardian, we struggled with trying to get our supply chain to work effectively. As I have shared earlier in this book, we tried to outsource this function, and then we took it back in-house because third parties can only handle high-value small-volume inventory, not the low-value high-volume inventory that a pharmacy chain handles every day.

The key functions of any supply chain in most retail companies can be divided into three segments:

Inventory

For a retail store or chain, the inventory it carries and the rate at which it has purchased the inventory make all the difference between profits and losses. Managing this inventory is the key challenge every supply chain manager will face as his primary task. Too much stocking resulting in locked cash or very low margins resulting in an impact on the bottom line will both prove to be a challenge for every retail chain.

The Guardian proprietary master database has over 65,000 active SKUs and we add over five hundred products to it every month. Managing an inventory with such a large number of SKUs spread across several cities in many states is a big challenge.

Each time we opened a new store, we found that we would ship stocks based on what we thought a store should have, rather than conducting a quick research in the locality and then sending out the stocks. This resulted in unnecessary and slow-moving stocks being sent to stores. It took many months for us to understand that these stocks were slow-moving and an even longer time to bring these back to our warehouse for return or reallocation.

There are several aspects of inventory for a pharmacy retail chain that need to be addressed by every entrepreneur, irrespective of which line of business one may be attempting to build one's dream in.

Purchasing: The age-old adage for purchasing is to buy the right product in the right quantity at the right price. What is 'right' has to be defined by the supply chain manager who is responsible for this activity.

Getting an honest purchase manager is a dream for any retail company and I have been generally fortunate in this aspect, though we have also been forced to ask some people in the purchase function to leave because we found that they had compromised the interests of the company.

When I started Guardian, I had so many things to address that I was not able to handle centralized buying. We, therefore, allowed stores to buy directly from suppliers. Before I knew it, we had over two thousand suppliers, out of which over 90 per cent were giving us less than ₹10,000 worth of goods in one year. These suppliers would call at all odd hours of the day demanding payment of a few thousand rupees and they refused to honour their commitment of taking back the expired stocks.

The other issue, as a result of multiple suppliers, was a huge inventory build-up. Our people had ordered goods not because these would sell in our stores but because they happened to know the medical representative and were helping this individual meet his weekly or monthly sales targets. This was compounded because we had multiple people ordering stocks at various stores.

We have now centralized all purchases at our head office so that there is little or no leeway available to store staff to exercise their own discretion, either to introduce new products or new suppliers. Given the width of the chain and depth of our inventory requirement, we have also had to provide for local purchase at different warehouses to cater to the indigenously manufactured drugs that are prescribed by the local doctors.

As soon as we centralized our purchases, we saw our margins move up significantly. We were buying more and therefore our negotiating ability was much better. More importantly, we discovered that our buying margins for the same product varied significantly across cities and suppliers. We implemented a system of taking the lowest cost supplier and buying from him for the entire chain.

At Guardian, we have category managers who are responsible not just for purchases but also for margins. In addition to better buying, they have to ensure that the stock levels in each category are as per the agreed norms and budgets. They are also charged with the responsibility of moving stocks from one store to another if there is excess stock in one place and a shortage at another.

The purchase function at Guardian also has one more important role—to ensure that urgent requirements at the stores, such as products needed immediately by a customer, are delivered quickly.

Old and slow-moving inventory: Inventory has this incredible ability to get old and the more it is handled, either by the store staff or the customer, the less it is likely to get sold! As inventory gets older, its value drops and even the manufacturers resist taking it back.

Guardian too has had its fair share of problems with old and slow-moving inventory and we are learning from our experience. I have seen old inventory piled up in store corners because the store staff is either too lazy to send it back or just does not care. When I insisted on having it sent back to the warehouse, I was shocked to find that the warehouse had created a separate section to receive such inventory. The inventory which should have been returned to the supplier for a full cash refund was literally being dumped in the warehouse resulting in losses.

As a result of this poor inventory management, we had to

write off inventory worth crores of rupees because we did not manage the aging process of the inventory well. We should have sold older inventory first and as it approached expiry we should have returned this to the warehouse for a refund from the suppliers. In our early days, writing off inventory was always a very painful exercise for me because I could see my hard-earned investment flying out of the window. Though we now have much stronger systems to manage our stocks we still face losses due to poor execution. I have now managed to internalize this fact and have accepted these costs as a part of the business.

Expired products: The pharmacy trade is fortunate in that we are able to return all our expired and near-expiry medicines to the distributors, who in turn return these products to the manufactures. While this facility exists, most chemists are not able to return all their expired and slow-moving medicines because of poorly managed stores and inefficient management of stocks. As a result of this, these chemists have to incur losses. These losses can only be ascribed to poor inventory control at the retail shop or at the warehouse.

First in first out: In order to manage the inventory of a retail pharmacy chain, it is absolutely essential to follow the very simple 'first in first out' sales principle. However, this proves to be easier said than done. Medicines need to be tracked by their expiry date as well as batch number and in our early days, I found that sales were either done without keeping track of the batch number, or incorrect batch numbers were entered for the product. This led to complete chaos in our inventory. Products in the store did not match with the products in the system, showing excess in the system and shortfall when the physical verification was done.

It took us several months to introduce barcoding, which is the only way to manage the batch number and expiry date of inventory. We have looked at higher-level technologies such as radio frequency identification devices (RFID), but have found these to be far too expensive for a pharmacy chain, where the average ticket size is very small.

Warehouse

Managing a warehouse or a distribution centre for a retail company is a very challenging task. Not only are we required to receive and dispatch the inventory, we also have to ensure that the stocks are stocked properly and the dispatch is done in accordance with a plan and not in a haphazard manner.

No one likes returns but this is a process that has to be completed each month, every month. The warehouse is responsible for sending all the expired and slow-moving goods back to suppliers, who always resist taking back stocks, since this has a direct impact on their sales each month.

We manage multiple warehouses in different states to service the requirements of stores in each city. This has to be done to save the multipoint tax that is levied in our country across state borders. Small warehouses are inefficient and much more expensive to run.

With the impending introduction of the Goods and Services Tax in the country, I am hoping to close all these small warehouses and building one large warehouse to supply all our stores in the National Capital Region. With improving infrastructure, one warehouse could supply to all our stores in North India as well.

Logistics

While delivering inventory from the warehouse to the store seems to be an easy task, when one starts looking at the thousands of products that have to be delivered to hundreds of stores, the complexity of the matter multiplies manifold. We had to learn how to deliver a few strips of medicines to a store that was more than fifty miles away, simply because we had not planned our regular supply properly.

Managing a fleet of vehicles was a nightmare for our logistics manager. He would dispatch the vans to the stores based on a preset route plan but he would find that the driver had decided to exercise his own initiative, resulting in all the optimization coming to naught.

In the beginning I gave the reasons why we stopped using our own vehicles. I have not found an answer to the 'lease versus buy' decision for commercial vehicles required to deliver products.

To make matters worse, since jobs are easily available and the salary differentiation is not significant, drivers walk away without any notice or simply don't come to work the following day.

We were also faced with a lot of stock missing between the time the goods left the warehouse and were delivered to stores. The dispatcher, the recipient and the driver would all swear that they had absolutely no idea where the goods had disappeared. We were never able to come to a decision and most of the times we ended up paying the price.

We are now trying out ways to lock the boxes that are sent to the warehouse, but locks tend to break in transit, plastic containers reach without lids, and no one seems to know who did it or how it happened!

My learning over the last few years has been that unless the lowest common denominator in the organization, which for Guardian is the 'picker' at the warehouse and the 'customer-care executive' at the store, accepts the value of the supply chain and starts to handle the inventory entrusted to his care properly, no amount of inventory planning and spreadsheet analysis at senior management level will help improve supply of goods.

Dealing with Suppliers

A few years back, while speaking to the senior managers of a few of the leading fast-moving consumer goods companies at a conference in Goa, I said that the relationship between the manufacturer and the retailer is starting to change. They could no longer dump stocks at the end of each quarter. I told them, 'The modern retailer is as educated as you and as well trained as you. He can think like you and can talk like you.'

These companies were used to dealing with small stores where they could push their stocks at the end of each month, quarter or year. In recognition of this change, most FMCGs have now set up a separate department to deal with retailers.

When we started operations, for the first few years, purchases were initially made through distributors because the manufacturers of these products were not willing to deal directly with me. Sales heads of companies would not be willing to meet me. If I did manage to get past the receptionist or their secretary—who wanted to know, 'What is the nature of your business'—and through to the concerned manager, they would quickly say, 'Let me get back to you' or 'I will send my medical representative to meet you.'

If I did manage to get an appointment, they would ask me to meet them at their convenience with no regard for mine. And

I was all along under the impression that we were the buyers and they were the suppliers!

There was one instance when I tried to meet the head of a leading beauty company. He did give me time to meet him but refused to discuss any business since 'your business is so small that it does not warrant my time'. When we signed three large stores at the new international and domestic airports in New Delhi airport, he was the first person to call and said, 'When can you send me your store drawings so that I can mark out which shelves I would be taking for our company's products?'

As our purchases started to get bigger, we gave our suppliers full access to the data pertaining to the sale of their stocks in each store and they reciprocated by giving us better margins and announcing special schemes for our customers, exclusively at our stores.

INFORMATION TECHNOLOGY
AND BUSINESS ANALYTICS

We know that, when it comes to technology and the economy,
if you're not constantly moving forward,
then—without a doubt—you're moving backwards.

—Bill Owens

I have always been a great believer in using information technology to improve our productivity. I have ensured that no costs are spared on keeping Guardian's technology requirements up to date. We have invested heavily in technology to manage our chain of stores and continue to upgrade this on a regular basis.

Software

While taking a decision on which software to use, I had to plan ahead and think big. When we started Guardian, I was not aware of what we needed or what software platform would work. We looked at some of the bigger names in retail software and realized that we could not afford their solutions.

At the same time, I realized that the pharmacy business needed different parameters. While all retailers needed to manage two parameters, maximum retail price (MRP) and expiry date, we needed to manage three parameters under law— MRP, expiry date and batch number. These added significantly to the complexity of our operations.

The point of sale software we use is very user friendly. Looking ahead, we are looking at the possibility of moving to a more robust platform such as Oracle or SAP.

Pirated Software

Having worked for three global companies, I recognize the serious problem of pirated software. I was very clear that Guardian would never use any pirated software. The temptation to use it in our country, as in several other countries, I am sure is huge, simply because of its easy availability and low cost. But I have issued very clear instructions to my IT colleagues, 'If you ever see any pirated software installed on any company-owned computer, please format the entire hard disk, irrespective of how much data there is on the computer or how important the data is for the company.'

The store staff would be held accountable for the loss of any data because of the formatting of their store computer hard disk. Only the strictest action would have ensured compliance with this directive and I know that no pirated software is knowingly used on any computer owned by Guardian.

Barcoding

Retail companies can best manage their huge inventories with barcoding if the value per unit is small because higher-level technologies like RFID are too expensive for us to use.

At Guardian, too, we tried to implement barcoding. While we were able to do so for all goods which came with manufacturer-printed barcodes, we realized that our largest business segment, medicines, had no barcodes at all. The pharmaceutical industry in India has not thought it important to barcode all their medicines and even today, despite many requests, medicines are possibly the only items that are not barcoded in our country.

In order to implement barcodes, we had to get Guardian registered with the authorities so that we could start printing our own barcodes. Each barcode is linked to the batch number, the MRP and the expiry date of each unit, and there is a high possibility of getting ten boxes of the same medicine from the supplier with different batch numbers, though with the same MRP and expiry date.

Printing the barcode was a simple exercise. Fixing them on our products was a huge challenge, since we had to paste thousands of barcodes on strips, tubes and bottles of medicine.

When we tried this exercise eight years back, we had inexperienced staff and found that there were many pasting errors. In addition, a number of customers would come into our store and ask for 'cut strips' since they only wanted a few tablets. If the strip was not cut correctly or if the portion with the barcode was handed over to the customer, the remaining medicine strip became unusable since there was no way to identify which batch it belonged to. Sometimes the barcode of one medicine was pasted on to another, leading to utter confusion at our stores. This resulted in plenty of irate customers who thought we had overcharged them on purpose. Though I stopped the barcoding exercise immediately and we went back to the old system, the process of removing the barcodes and correcting the prices proved to be a big challenge.

Three years later, when the warehouse staff had matured and the company's need for managing inventory had grown significantly, we restarted barcoding the medicines. This time the process worked well because we set up a quality control cell in each warehouse to ensure that the pasting was done correctly

The pharmaceutical industry has still not implemented barcoding, once again establishing that the industry continues to believe that the doctors are its customers and not the people who buy their medicines.

In-Store Video Cameras

With a couple of years of starting Guardian, we started to see that pilferage at some stores had started to increase. Since a pharmacy's format is small, it does not lend itself to large overheads for managing stocks or ensuring daily checks on cash. At the same time, customers often don't insist on a bill for their purchases. This leads to store staff taking some of the unbilled cash, since we cannot physically check all the inventories every day.

As hardware prices dropped and the cost of bandwidth became affordable, I decided to install two video cameras in our larger stores on a trial basis. One camera covers the cash desk and the area around the cashier and the other covers the exit door, along with some of the aisles or shelves. The video images from these cameras are captured on the hard disc of the store computers and these are reviewed regularly by the company's loss prevention teams.

The moment we had these cameras installed, we found a significant reduction in pilferage. Store staff now knew that they were being watched. We have caught them attempting to steal cash or stocks on camera and we have taken strong deterrent action. This message has spread through the company very quickly and the store staff has since become more vigilant.

We also installed video cameras inside our warehouses and outside our hospital stores. These cameras send live feed to the head office twenty-four hours and I have often seen our senior operations leadership watching a camera and calling the store to find out why the customer queue is long, or calling a warehouse to ask why goods are lying on the floor and not stacked on their respective shelves. Video cameras have now become standard fixtures as a part of each new store's fit-out plan.

Moving Forward

The information technology needs of a growing company will continue to rise exponentially, and the entrepreneur and IT head must always be one step ahead in thinking through the requirements of the organization.

At Guardian, we constantly upgrade our software and hardware in keeping with the growing needs of the company. Over the next year, we will start migrating all our systems to the SAP or Oracle platform, which will help us manage our growing business much better and will serve our needs for information technology well into the future.

Analysing the Numbers

Most businesses leave the work-related numbers in the monthly profit and loss account and balance sheet to the CFO. However, financial numbers are generally used to do a post-mortem of the performance while daily analytics are necessary to 'course correct' on an ongoing basis, every day.

I had to work hard on understanding our operating numbers and performance metrics since most managers are not keen to work with numbers, partly because they are uncomfortable with them and partly because they are unsure of what these numbers will reveal.

From simple analysis to inter-store analysis to detailed

analysis of revenue per square foot to yield per square foot of running shelf space, we have worked on all areas of business analytics. This data has helped us develop operating norms to determine how a store is performing, as well as to set up guidelines for new stores.

Our financial controller now heads the data group of the company. With his penchant for numbers, he has started bringing in a lot of sanity to the way the entire organization looks at numbers. He has also been empowered to look at any metrics and after due analysis he sends queries to the concerned functional/business head.

This manager reports directly to the CEO. This reporting relationship has communicated the importance the organization accords to data analysis.

With regard to business analytics, the challenges we faced was to convince everyone to look at our numbers and focus on the same set of conclusions. I found it was easier to get people to start using analytics when we asked them to look at numbers in business terms to address a problem. For example, when I asked our retail pharmacy business head to compare the revenue per square foot of stores in similar localities to understand why one store was performing better than another, we were able to get quick results.

I had asked my colleagues to produce reports and circulate them to all senior managers, but I found that most people were not even bothering to look at these. I then asked some senior colleagues to define the reports they wanted to see, rather than the IT department determining what they should see. We suddenly noticed an increase in the use of the data being generated every day.

Implementation of analytics in any organization will take

time. Getting our managers to start reading simple reports was a bigger challenge than getting them to understand more complex reports. Once they had understood the value of the simple reports, their hunger for data started to increase exponentially. I now find that our presentations have significantly higher number-based analysis.

We have also been working on analysing our inventory in more ways than one and this understanding is helping us to optimize our inventory, resulting in releasing precious cash for the company.

CONSULTANTS–KEEP THEM ONLY AS CONSULTANTS

Buddha left a road map, Jesus left a road map, Krishna left
a road map [...]
But you still have to travel the road yourself.

—Stephen Levine, poet

Like all other entrepreneurs, I too worked with a selection of consultants, which is why I now have at least a dozen unread reports in my office, gathering dust. It took me a while and reasonable sums of money before I understood that compensation of consultants should be linked directly to results. The moment I steered a conversation with a consultant to success-fee-based compensation, I would see the light and the enthusiasm go out of his eyes.

I must state that our experience with the consultants we selected or the consultants we could afford was generally poor. I am not suggesting that all experiences with consultants would fall into the same groove.

Most of the consultants I worked with were unwilling to 'roll up their sleeves' and come into the pit to work with us. They were ready to give advice or cheer from the outside, though. I don't think I have ever come across any consultant who turned around and told me that something was not possible or feasible.

This narrative would be incomplete without sharing some of the stories about our consultants.

Management and Marketing Consultant

I once brought in a senior consultant since he had almost thirty years of experience in running some of the major pharmaceutical companies in India. He claimed to have significant experience in pharmaceutical marketing and to have launched some of the biggest brands in the country. His resume showed that he had worked for a number of large pharmaceutical companies in India, that too, at very senior levels.

I had little knowledge of this sector then and believed him, though I should have done my own research. My brief to him was to train store staff and improve our customer service levels and to work towards increasing footfall in our stores. In addition, he was mandated to introduce our procurement head to the sales heads of various companies in the pharmaceutical industry to increase our margins.

When it came to reviewing his performance, he had a file full of excuses, which essentially blamed my management team for his failures.

I fired him.

Supply Chain Consultant

At Guardian, we have faced a lot of challenges in managing our supply chain, like any other retail company which has to deliver thousands of units to hundreds of stores. The pharmacy business is more complex since we have to deliver small SKUs (Stock Keeping Units), like a single strip of medicine, to multiple locations. This makes the management of the supply chain a major challenge.

After many false starts and meetings with advisors, consultants and supply chain specialists, we were approached by a group of individuals who claimed that they would be able to significantly improve our supply chain efficiencies. My brief to them was simple: improve fill rates and ensure inventories don't go out of line.

These consultants spent almost one year with us. They experimented with our stores, with our inventory and with our systems. They told us to set reorder levels at all stores and when we asked them to set these levels, they brought in another set of consultants! This meant more costs.

Finally, after increasing our inventory levels from a healthy forty-five days to a not-so-healthy ninety days, which resulted in doubling the amount of money locked in stocks and reducing our fill rates, they recommended that Guardian should hire a senior supply chain professional and outsource the entire supply chain to a third-party professional logistics and warehousing company.

We decided to follow their advice. Nothing went right from the first day. A third party to manage your supply chain can only work if you have high value SKUs that can be delivered by courier and where deliveries are done on a lower frequency. At a pharmacy warehouse, goods are being delivered round the clock and sometimes we may even have to deliver a few strips of medicines to a store.

Before we knew it, the newly hired supply chain head and the outsourcing agency were at loggerheads with one another because the supply chain head wanted to have his own way by managing stocks directly and the outsourcing agency did not want to lose their contract and therefore opposed the new supply chain head in everything, while supplies to the stores suffered. Customers started complaining because they were not getting the required medicines at our stores.

This experiment had gone horribly wrong and we were back to building the supply chain from scratch. We took the entire supply chain operations back under our own control and decided to manage it internally this time.

Financial Consultants

Like any young retail company, our need for funds was large and I knew that this requirement would increase as the chain continued to expand.

Working with the nationalized banking system in our country is always a challenge. Private and multinational banks don't normally like to lend money to young companies and startups.

Over the past few years, we have worked with many consultants who have promised to raise working capital facilities, term loans and non-fund-based facilities. Some of them have been recommended by the very bankers who were supposed to receive the loan application, and claimed access to the highest level of every bank. When I would try to explain that our proposal should be able to stand on its own merit, their standard response would be, 'You have no idea how complex fundraising is.'

Then they would pull out a detailed application form, which needed to be completed for submission to each bank that we wished to approach for funds. I was in no position to complete these forms, given all my other commitments, and so I had no choice but to go along.

Not one of these self-styled financial consultants were able to deliver. Our working capital facilities were set up only after the finance head and I started interacting directly with the bankers. Getting to know the bankers was a very important move that I made more by default than by design, thanks to a number of inept consultants. This relationship with bankers has served me very well in the last six years.

Private Label Consultant

One of our stated policies is to build the Guardian private label.

Private labels are necessary for every retail chain, to increase margins as well as to bring people back to the stores. As we started the process, we were naturally approached by a group of people who claimed to be experts in private label development. Knowing full well that the concept of private labels in the pharmacy business was new and that Guardian would be pioneering such an initiative in India, I still decided to engage one of them.

This person took a mandate for three months and agreed to do a review with us every Friday morning at 10 a.m. The first few weeks were spent in expressing niceties of how well-integrated the Guardian management team was, and so on. Once we started asking for additional inputs and feedback on the various researches that he was supposedly conducting, he brought a twenty-one-year-old trainee who, he said, was his assistant and an 'expert' in private labels.

The conclusion that was drawn after so many months of research was that since Guardian was not 'protecting' its pharmacy brand name properly, there was no reason to believe that we would be able to protect a private label brand. In addition, they picked out some of the products that we had planned to launch and checked how much were our sales in those categories.

Since most of these categories were new, our stores showed

zero sales statistics for these products and competing products in the same category. Our consultant interpreted these numbers to mean zero demand and hence zero potential. When we launched some of these products, in spite of his negative recommendations, they became runaway hits.

'Statutory' Consultants

I use the word 'statutory' consultants because we needed a knowledgeable 'middleman' for virtually every statutory matter that has to be addressed by most companies in our country. When anything runs into a problem, everyone's immediate reaction is to call the consultant so that he can 'fix' matters. This list includes consultants for employee provident fund and employee state insurance, sales tax and value added tax, import of goods, income tax matters, the various returns under the Companies Act and for the elaborate paperwork required under the Income Tax Act.

We have also worked with consultants for handling matters under the Drugs and Cosmetics Act, the Weights and Measurements Act and the Shops and Establishment Act.

An interesting incident took place when we started selling personal weighing machines at our stores. An inspector fined us because we had not complied with the Weights and Measurements Act of the country. The fine was at the rate of ₹5,000 for each director of the company. We paid a fine of ₹30,000 to sell a weighing scale worth ₹1,000.

We realized that we needed a licence to sell weighing machines, and that too, a separate one for every store. The cost of the licence for all our stores was greater than our annual sales revenue from weighing scales, so we decided that Guardian would not sell them, even though we sold products to lose weight! The logic of the legislation was to control traders who would cheat innocent consumers by selling them products that weighed less than what was claimed. However, this noble intention of our lawmakers was completely mismanaged when it was interpreted as a law applicable to personal weighing scales.

When I discussed this with my friend, who is a hotelier, he laughed and said that his company had been battling this with the Weights and Measurements Department for many years since under the law, they needed over three thousand licenses—one for every weighing scale placed in every hotel room!

There was another matter where we needed to hire a consultant for something that I assumed was ours by right. In January 2009, we purchased land in an auction conducted by the Debt Recovery Tribunal of India through the Delhi High Court. I bought this land to construct our corporate office and it had to be transferred to our company's name.

This simple process of transferring the land was been held up with the authorities for over eighteen months, simply because I had been resisting the appointment of a consultant recommended by the authorities. I was advised that as soon as I agreed to hire the consultant, the transfer of the land would be done within one week. I agreed to this and we managed to get the land registered by the end of 2011.

Foreign Consultants

I met a couple of senior managers who had spent over two decades in pharmacy retail in the US. They assured me that they would be able to help with my supply chain and merchandising problems. Though I had some reservations about their ability to work in Indian conditions, I had very few options, so I decided to engage them to help me strengthen Guardian's operations.

The engagement letter they sent me outlined their scope of work and encompassed the areas where they were going to assist me:

- Competitor virtues, values and vulnerabilities
- Format design, including location choice, street appeal, colours, building materials and signing
- Merchandising, including fixtures, fixture colours and internal store shopping patterns
- Product category assortments from high level to subcategory
- HR management, staffing and training at stores and corporate headquarters
- Merchandising strategy
- Marketing, advertising and promotion
- Product sourcing and supply chain issues
- Pricing—everyday and promotional
- Information technology and financial systems and support
- Legal and regulatory issues
- Risks to be managed and ways to manage them
- Security issues throughout the business
- Cultural issues important to the business
- Corporate organizational structure and culture
- Visioning plans of Reliance, Pantaloon, Walmart, Bharti and others

The points listed above covered everything that a CEO would be expected to do along with his team and I should have realized that no consultant could supervise such a vast scope of subjects without trying to run the company himself.

We engaged two of these consultants, since they said that they would be more effective as a team, at US$ 2,000 per head per day. In addition, we had to meet the costs of hotels and chauffeur-driven cars in India, plus business-class air fares from USA.

Their first assignment was for a period of ten days, which was a study trip. They studied our operations and made us pay for it.

Their second trip was for another ten days, and this time they came with a set of recommendations that they asked us to implement so that they could review our implementation skills. None of the points listed in their scope of work was covered after almost twenty days of work. They had not even got started and we had run up bills worth almost $100,000.

By the time they started to plan their third visit, I was at my wits' end on how to stop this expense. Finally, I called them and said that there was no need for them to come and that we would reestablish contact when we needed them.

My learning after using such consultants was that most of the answers a company needs are available in-house with the management. Internal brainstorming throws up much better solutions to problems, with a much higher possibility of a management buy-in, than what an external resource can come up with.

BUILD AN ORGANIZATION WITH INTEGRITY, ETHICS AND HONESTY

It is a man's own mind, not his enemy or foe, that lures him to evil ways.

—Gautama Buddha

L aying the foundation of an honest organization, built with strong integrity and ethics, is important to set the culture, direction and priorities for any new company.

The lead has to be taken by the promoter of the company, by setting the right example and standards.

Honesty Is Black or White—There Is No Grey

To me, honesty is a simple black and white choice. There is neither grey in honesty, nor are there any shades of white and black, as I have heard many people say. Either you are honest or dishonest.

I told both my sons when they were leaving home to pursue their education overseas that every morning when they looked in the mirror, if they were able to look themselves in the eye and tell themselves, 'I did no wrong yesterday and I did not knowingly harm anyone yesterday,' that is the only explanation they would ever need to give. What anyone else thought of them or their actions was of no relevance. My advice was, 'If someone doesn't like the way you handle something, hear them out, but you don't have to implement their idea. You can't please everyone.'

The Leader Sets the Standard in Honesty

Integrity, ethics and honesty can only be implemented in a company through personal example. It is also essential to set the right standards from the beginning.

If I had started a culture of taking free medicines from my company or if I had asked stores to send cash to me from the cash box or pulled cash out of the company, I would not have been able to demonstrate the right leadership values, and there would have been no way for me to implement a strong code of conduct in the company. To this day, I highlight every personal entertainment and other such expenses on my credit card statement, as well as every international personal phone call, and pay for it separately from my own account.

When I speak to our young store staff, I always tell them that their parents, like every parent in the world, must have taught them three basic values, 'Don't lie, don't steal and fear God.'

No parent would teach his child to lie, to steal or to not fear God, irrespective of their religious beliefs. Yet, all retail companies, including Guardian, are faced with theft of products from our stores and warehouses. While we take strong disciplinary action against anyone caught stealing, I have not been able to understand what is it that leads a young person at the start of his professional life to steal? What drives a person to take something that does not belong to him?

From our early days, I remember one incident very clearly. I was standing near the cash counter of our first store at Galleria.

A smart lady in her mid-thirties walked into the store and picked up some shampoos, soaps, cosmetics, health products and a few more items. She walked up to the counter and I could see that my pharmacist behind the counter was excited, because her total purchase could have represented a large part of our daily sales in our first store. She put all these items on the counter, took out her credit card and said very matter-of-factly, 'Give me all these products, but make a bill for antibiotic capsules and other medicines.'

The income tax laws in India permit ₹15,000 a year to be claimed as tax-free medical reimbursement. Most companies add this amount in the overall compensation package and in order to recover the 'tax-free' money that is a part of their total salary package, many people have to resort to submitting 'fake' medical bills.

My colleague knew my views on this but he still looked at me, and I shook my head. He could see the sale flying away, but he responded, 'Sorry madam, at Guardian we can only give you a bill for what you purchase.'

This angered her and she started to shout at the store staff, saying that she had never seen such a 'useless' store and that her neighbourhood chemist would always give her a bill for what she wanted. She stormed out of the store and we put the products back on the shelves. A few days later, she visited the store again and asked for some medicines. I walked up to her and said, 'Madam, we will not be able to give you a bill for anything other than what you have purchased.'

Her response was heart-warming and gave me the confidence that the path I had started to walk on was indeed the correct one for Guardian. 'If you don't give fake bills, I am confident you don't sell fake medicines,' she said. She has been a loyal customer ever since.

It is very difficult to say 'no' when you are confronted with an ethical issue, but the cost of saying 'yes' will prove to be huge in the future. It is always better to say 'no' now if you don't agree on a point than to face the consequences later.

Threshold of Conscience

I have often argued with colleagues and others about whether using a company car to drop one's children to school or take one's wife shopping, to charge a personal expense as official entertainment or to convert a business-class ticket into two economy tickets when travelling overseas on company work so that your partner can fly free, is right or wrong. These are examples of when we alter our threshold of conscience and accept an action that we would normally not allow from our subordinates. We would also not see any of this as correct if we heard of someone else doing something similar.

I learned to accept that I am nobody to decide what is right and wrong on behalf of someone else, since this is a pure value judgment call. As long as my own conscience is clear and as long as I know that I am doing what I think is right, I will keep moving forward.

I have always maintained my own sense of integrity, ethics and honesty in my dealings as per my threshold of conscience, though I know I have also learned to look the other way if I see someone else following practices that do not agree with mine.

I have recognized that very often, in order to get work done, I have to accept the normal pattern of working in our country. I have also learned not to question why, at most times, 'favours' need to be given to even get what is yours by right and not because you are asking for something to be done that is incorrect or out of turn.

A senior bureaucrat from a Southeast Asian country once told me that there was no corruption in his homeland. They believed in the philosophy of cooperation, not corruption. 'If you are going to do business in my country and make a profit, you need to cooperate and share a part of this profit with us,' he said.

Gifting is another area where there are several shades of grey. In our country, it is almost a culture to give gifts on Diwali every year and if a present is not accepted, it is seen as an affront by the giver. Yet, if the recipient makes it abundantly clear that gifts are not welcome, then the practice of giving gifts would come to a stop.

At Guardian, we receive a lot of gifts from our suppliers. Our policy is the same: all gifts must be received only in the head office of the company. They are recorded by the administrative department. At the annual company dinner, we hold a lucky draw for all staff members and distribute these gifts.

CORPORATE SOCIAL RESPONSIBILITY

Corporate social responsibility is a hard-edged business decision. Not because it is a nice thing to do or because people are forcing us to do it...because it is good for our business.

—Niall FitzGerald, former co-chairman and CEO, Unilever

At Guardian, we have always attempted to meet our corporate social responsibility through various means. Some of these are:

Wellness camps: Guardian conducts camps in association with various pharmaceutical companies and local NGOs to address the health needs of the community our stores serve. Some of the camps that Guardian conducts regularly inside residential complexes and office communities are for management of diabetes, understanding cardiac problems, understanding and managing stress, managing asthma, cessation of smoking, basic first-aid including artificial resuscitation, and weight management, diet and nutrition.

Pulse polio vaccine: Some years back we were approached by the local government to work with them to deliver the polio vaccine every few months. We now open up our stores each time the government of India runs a campaign. The vaccine has been administered to thousands of children at our stores.

Free medicines: Cut strips are normally a source of wastage for most pharmacies. Guardian hands over cut strips of medicines on a regular basis to local NGOs so that these can be used for patients who cannot afford to buy them. We have also contributed free medicines during all national emergencies like the earthquakes, terrorist attacks and floods.

Guardian scholar award: Our company has instituted merit-based Guardian scholarships at leading pharmacy colleges in the states that we operate in. This has helped us get the Guardian brand more recognition among young graduates and has also helped recruit some excellent managers for the company.

As a part of our corporate social responsibility, we also support patients below the poverty line in hospitals where we have Guardian stores. If a patient is not able to pay his or her hospital bills, we waive the bill for medicines as well.

PERSONAL LIFE AND HEALTH

There are six components of wellness: proper weight and diet, proper exercise, breaking the smoking habit, control of alcohol, stress management and periodic exams.

—Kenneth H. Cooper

Don't Let Your Mind Give Up

So many battles are lost if the mind accepts defeat or gives up too easily.

When I chat with entrepreneurs who started a venture but gave it up or professionals who conceded defeat in a corporate battle for supremacy, I know that they gave up the fight because they had not built the internal resilience in their minds to stay the course. It's like a game of golf where one plays much better when the mind is at rest.

I have found that giving up is very easy and several times in my own journey, both as a professional as well as an entrepreneur, I have had the temptation to call it a day because all choices seemed to be tough and insurmountable. As I look back on my life, I wonder what kind of a person I would have been had I given up each time my body told me to stop.

The joy of completing a task that once seemed impossible has its own high.

Don't Lose Sight of Your Personal Life

As a professional manager, I had always encouraged my colleagues to take leave every year. Whenever someone told me that he was working over twelve hours a day on a regular basis, my response was, 'If you cannot finish your allotted work during office hours, you are either overworked and need an assistant or very inefficient.'

Similarly, when someone told me that he had not taken any leave for so many years, my response would be, 'You have not done the company a favour. I would like you to take your leave and come back to work rejuvenated.'

I have never refused any manager his leave whenever he has asked for it.

Many entrepreneurs tell me that they don't have the time to take a vacation and I have never believed any of them. As a professional manager I did not stay late and as an entrepreneur, I try to leave my office by 6.30 every evening. It took me a while to explain to my colleagues at Guardian that I did not expect them to stay in office simply because I was still sitting in my room. At the same time, I have managed to convey to all my colleagues that while I don't expect them to work late, I definitely expect them to complete the work that they have committed to finish before they go home.

If a person cannot take time off for himself and give his mind and body a rest, then there is a problem brewing in the long run. I have always taken my vacation every year, irrespective of the work pressure.

A decade back, I could afford to switch off completely while we were on a vacation. Excuses like, 'I am sorry, I was not able to get through' or 'the fax or telex you sent me was garbled', were acceptable then. However, today, in the age of mobile phones and high-speed Internet access in every hotel room, while I do try and switch off from work, I have no choice but to stay connected to my office and my colleagues all the time.

Vera had also established another rule at home—every night, we would have dinner together at 9 p.m. at the family dining table, irrespective of what anyone's plans were. This gave us an opportunity to spend time with one another and when the boys were younger, dinner conversations would be something I used to look forward to, since this was a time when they would share their day's highs and lows. Even today, when both our sons come home on vacation, we follow this practice. Even if the boys have planned an evening out with their friends, they make sure they sit with us for dinner before going out.

When I hear my friends tell me that they never have time to 'eat together as a family', I feel sorry for what they are missing.

As I worked on building Guardian, I found that dinnertime conversations with Vera and my sons, when they were visiting home during vacations, was a good opportunity to let off steam and vent my frustrations of the day. Yet another practice we have followed consistently is to pray together at all festivals.

Manage Personal Health Well

Work pressure while building any new business will be intense and an entrepreneur has no choice but to stay well and stay fit. He needs to build the stamina to keep going, in the face of all possible adversity. Falling sick is not an option that can be considered.

There will be many moments when every entrepreneur wants to throw in the towel simply because the stress becomes unbearable, yet unlike any other individual, it is important to keep going because the light at the end of the tunnel is the achievement of his dream.

Over the past few years, either because of my increasing age or because of my genes or because of simple work-related stress that I probably have but don't care to show, my blood pressure has been slightly high and a couple of years back I discovered I was mildly diabetic. I could have slowed down because of blood pressure and diabetes but I chose not to accept these as anything more than another problem that could be managed.

With a regular exercise regime and reasonable diet control, along with appropriate medication, I have managed to control both my blood pressure and my diabetes to within acceptable levels.

Build Internal Resilience and Stay Calm

No matter how much stress you may carry inside you, it is very important to 'appear' absolutely calm from the outside. It is essential for anyone embarking on a journey to build strong internal resilience. Every entrepreneur has to develop a thick skin and learn to accept all kinds of comments about himself and his company. Developing the ability to stay calm in the face of adversity is an important quality that has served me well. Let me recount some instances

In 1994 I had taken a train from Bhopal to New Delhi. I was sleeping in the upper berth of the train when, sometime in the middle of the night, I remember, almost in slow motion, rolling off the berth and falling on the floor. My briefcase, which was lying next to me, fell on top of my head. As I looked around, I was amazed to find the wreckage around me. People were screaming and shouting and several must have been seriously injured. The train bogey was lying on its side. All the lights of the compartment had switched off. I struggled to stand on the grilled windows in the pitch darkness and managed to crawl out of the train. I then tried to help a few people recover their belongings and make the injured people comfortable.

More than fourteen hours later, a train arrived from New Delhi and the injured and other passengers were loaded inside like cattle. This experience helped me understand that when one is faced with a situation that one can do nothing about, it is better to take a deep breath and stay calm rather than react and do something that would harm one's own self and possibly others as well.

Develop the Ability to Sleep Anywhere

Sleep will become a very precious commodity for every individual wanting to start off on his or her own. Days and nights will blend into one. I sometimes don't realize when my day starts and ends.

I have often heard colleagues tell me that they are not able to sleep at night. My only advice to all of them is that losing sleep over a problem is not going to solve it. On the contrary, lack of proper sleep will make you unwell.

Every night, as my head hits my pillow, I am out like a light. Vera used to comment that she could not even have a proper fight with me because each time we started an argument, I would turn my head and go to sleep!

I always tell my colleagues and friends that they must develop the 'sleep anywhere' capability because sleep is the only true rest our bodies get. Over the past seven years, I have trained my body to sleep anywhere. I now take a power nap several times a day when I am in my car, going to work or for a meeting. I have learned how to sleep well on flights, buses and trains.

ACKNOWLEDGEMENTS

Over the last thirty-one years of our married life, we have moved fourteen homes across five cities and two countries. My wife Vera has always packed our bags, taken our boys and moved with me, no questions asked. She was a major anchor in my life as I built my career and pursued my dream. She single-handedly brought up our sons while I travelled across the globe in my capacity of a professional manager, sometimes for up to twenty days in a month. She is a no-nonsense individual with strong value systems, which she has also inculcated in our boys.

My sons, Varun and Ashwin, have always given me their unstinted support on virtually everything, including when I started Guardian Pharmacy. I don't remember any doubts being raised by either of them, ever, on my plans to become an entrepreneur. Both were married in 2013 and our daughters-in-law, Ashwini and Gauravi, have also been very supportive of Guardian.

My father, Brigadier M.L. Garg, and my mother, Sudha Garg, questioned my plans of leaving a steady job in the corporate world, but later understood my reasons and stood by my decision. My in-laws, Captain Mahendra Agarwala and Bala Agarwala, encouraged me to go ahead with my goal of starting off on my own. My brothers, Atul and Kapil, and their wives, Parul and Ritu, also gave me unstinted support, investing some of their hard-earned money in the company.

My editor, Dibakar Ghosh, and my new publishers, Rupa Publications, have worked painstakingly to bring out this revised edition.

There are many people who have worked with me and so many more who have stood by me throughout my life. I express my sincerest thanks to everyone for having supported my dreams and my plans. I cannot name each of them individually, but based on all my interactions with them over the years, I am sure they all know that I am grateful to each one.